D0759953

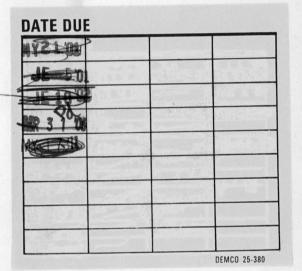

RIVERSIDE CITY COLLEGE
LIBRARY
Riverside, California

THE
AGE
FACTOR

THE AGE FACTOR

Love, Sex and Friendship in
Age-Different Relationships

Jack LaPatra, Ph. D.

M. EVANS and Company, Inc.
NEW YORK

Library of Congress Cataloging in Publication Data

LaPatra, Jack W   1927–
    The age factor.

    Includes bibliographical references.
    1. Interpersonal relations.   2. Marriage.   3. Age
groups.   I. Title.
HM132.L36   306.7   80-10349
ISBN 0-87131-312-X

M. Evans and Company, Inc.
216 East 49 Street
New York, New York 10017

Design by Robert Bull

Manufactured in the United States of America

9 8 7 6 5 4 3 2 1

Thanks are due to the following authors, publishers, and agents for permission to use the material included.

Pages 19–20: Grey Fox Press for an excerpt from *Gay Sunshine Interview* by Allen Young. Copyright © 1974 by Allen Young. Reprinted by permission of Grey Fox Press.

Pages 44, 48, 49, 55: Springer Publishing Company for material from *Love, Sex, and Marriage through the Ages* by Bernard I. Murstein. Copyright © 1974 by Springer Publishing Company, Inc., New York. Used by permission.

Pages 62, 63–64: The Sterling Lord Agency, Inc. for excerpts from "Marriage, Rational and Irrational" by Erica Jong (*Vogue*, June 1975). Copyright © 1975 Erica Jong. Reprinted by permission of The Sterling Lord Agency, Inc.

Pages 75, 77, 80–81: Harold Ober Associates for excerpts from *The New Years* by Anne Simon. Copyright © 1967, 1968 by Anne W. Simon. Reprinted by permission of Harold Ober Associates.

Page 83: Elsevier-Dutton Publishing Company, Inc. for an excerpt from *The Tao of Love and Sex: The Ancient Chinese Way to Ecstasy* by Jolan Chang. Copyright © 1977 by Jolan Chang. Reprinted by permission of the publisher, E. P. Dutton, and Wildwood House Ltd., London.

Pages 95–96: The Los Angeles Times Syndicate for an excerpt from "Dear Beth" by Beth Winship (*San Francisco Examiner & Chronicle*, 13 May 1977). Copyright © 1977 Los Angeles Times Syndicate. Reprinted with permission.

Pages 134–135: Harold Ober Associates for "Preference" from *Montage of a Dream Deferred* by Langston Hughes. Copyright © 1951 by Langston Hughes. Reprinted by permission of Harold Ober Associates.

To my dear friend, Emil White

CONTENTS

PREFACE

WE'VE ALL EXPERIENCED the mixed-up feelings that come when we're attracted to someone of a vastly different age. Remember the teacher we secretly loved, that fascinating older person we wanted for a friend, or the sweet young thing, male or female, who tugged at our heartstrings and stirred our genitals? What held us back from pursuing our desires? Were we convinced that such relationships were doomed to failure? Could we confront the self-doubt and social stigma that prevented us from developing rewarding relationships with other persons across the age-different barrier?

If you made a friend from across the generation gap, your coeval friends might say, "What do you see in that old man?" or "How do you talk to that kid?" And self-doubt hits you. You somehow doubt your happiness when others are uncomfortable because of it. You sense the envy of people titillated by your experience. You resent others for manufacturing explanations of

9

father worship, mama's boys, Oedipus complexes, gold diggers, and on and on to convince themselves that what you have isn't such a good deal after all. Our lives are enriched by our friends, lovers, and spouses. Requiring that these people have ages similar to ours never made much sense. We don't have to do that any more.

More and more Americans are challenging the age barrier, confronting the social stigma, learning to deal with their self-doubts, and enriching their lives with age-different relationships. Widowed older people find young lovers; disenchanted victims of coeval divorce try an age-different relationship the second time, men and women of all ages who feared the dangers of traditional marriage and delayed their unions now join in age-different marriages, and new styles of friendship flourish.

This book is not about the pairing habits of famous people. It is about typical Americans and their recognition that "the age factor" does not have to limit their choices. Agism, the discrimination against people on the basis of chronological age, hurts everyone. You are told to "act your age," but what should be said is "Act your stage." Successful relationships are formed based on matching developmental stages, and chronology may have little or nothing to do with our stage.

This book will show that there is nothing about age-different relationships that should persuade anyone to avoid them. Your attitudes, needs, stage of development, and goals may suggest that an age-different relationship is more suitable than an age-similar one. To discredit the possibility because of a stigma or for any other reason is to lose a rich alternative and limit your life options.

To explore the entire scope of the "breaking the age-different barrier" phenomenon would have been impossible without the open, candid sharing of many people. I am grateful for their gifts and will respect their anonymity.

I want to acknowledge the skillful help of Jane Jordan Browne, Enid Gruber, Susan Harte, Jane Holley Wilson, and Ann Baker. Their efforts helped make this book possible.

My loving thanks to my wife, Jesalee, who joined me on all of our interviews and with whom I share our age-different marriage. Her patient persistence helped me over the barrier.

Jack LaPatra
Atlanta

CHAPTER ONE

May-December Romances

I WILL ALWAYS remember Mr. Macintosh. He lived two blocks from me when I was growing up. His shabby house was surrounded by overgrown bushes, and he was rarely seen on the street.

Whenever he did appear, my friends and I froze at whatever we were doing and watched furtively until he was out of sight. When he had passed we went on with our play as though what had seized our attention was not discussible.

Mr. Macintosh was an old man, or so it seemed then. He always looked as though he had just been taken from a dusty shelf where he had been stored for years. He walked at a slow, steady pace, looking neither left nor right, and almost year-round wore a heavy black coat and a dark hat pulled low.

Mr. Macintosh sounds undistinguished enough, perhaps not even worth mentioning. On the contrary. Old Mr. Macintosh was married to a very young woman. I fear there is no way I can completely describe the impact that fact made on me as a boy. Fear, shame, incomprehension, curiosity, awe—all of these collided in my young sexual confusion.

Sometimes I would see Mrs. Macintosh hanging her wash to dry on the small windy hill behind their house. I could hardly breathe. My own adolescent sexual energy was powerful and confused, and the thought of an old man and a young woman making love overwhelmed me.

I now know that the Macintosh's marriage was based on a "May-December romance." Many youth of today will not know that quaint label, but it referred to a love affair between an older man and a younger woman, with or without marriage. Their age difference was usually twenty years or more.

My boyish view of marriage assumed people mated only for sex and children, and Mr. Macintosh, who looked and acted older than my grandfather, simply didn't jibe with that image. I also suspect that my attraction for the young and beautiful Mrs. Macintosh complicated my feelings.

Today I know a great deal about May-December romances from experience. As I sit here writing and recalling a boyhood memory of the Macintosh marriage, a few bars of a song drift in from the next room. They are hummed by my wife, Jesalee. She is twenty-two years younger than I am.

I know that our kind of May-December romance is more common than I earlier imagined, and that such alliances are increasing. And I also know that versions of Mr. Macintosh's shame and my confused response still persist.

Jesalee and I faced the barrier that society constructs to thwart age-different unions, and we took down the wall—brick by brick. I had more work to do than she. I had to deal with inner doubts and outer pressures. The doubts came from the thoughts that something must be wrong with me. Surely there was a sickness in my needs. And while self-doubt chewed at my innards, the questioning of friends and family created a feeling of isolation.

Most of those difficulties came from my own attitudes from the past, and eventually the awareness grew that all around us men and women were forming strong and happy age-different unions.

We and they love out in the open, undaunted by the self-doubt and stigma once attached to the May-December romance.

The visibility of May-December romances is higher than ever before. And I don't mean among the rich, famous, and eccentric. Men like Aristotle Onassis, Charlie Chaplin, Tommy Manville, and Henry Miller have always lived by a different code. I mean among fairly traditional American citizens of all sorts: widowed older people who find young mates; disenchanted victims of divorce who try an age-different relationship the second time; and men and women of all ages who feared the dangers of coeval marriage and delayed their couplings.

And these unions are remarkably successful. Romance, it seems, flourishes in the so-called gap between the generations.

Old prejudices die hard, though. As a culture we are still uneasy about age-different romances. Cautionary tales about the geriatric husband and his ripe, relentless bride abound. When an older man marries a young woman he must surely be senile, in his dotage, or simply a "dirty old man." The young woman must be after his money or neurotically seeking the father she never had.

Jokes reflecting these prejudices are told with gusto. Professional comic Lee Tully tells this one.

> I'm married to someone much younger than myself, and there are some problems. I have to get up every morning to take her to the school bus. Another problem is the different ages of our friends—hers are in Greenwich Village, mine in Retirement Village.[1]

There are many versions of the story about a recently divorced fiftyish man who had waited years to walk into his favorite restaurant with a beautiful young woman on his arm so that all of his friends would say, "Look at that lucky dog!"

When it finally happened he loved it until he overheard two diners referring to him not as a lucky dog, but rather as "a horny old goat." He immediately married the first middle-aged woman in his address book.

Age differences are no joke to the Salvation Army. Under the army's strict code, an officer's wife may not be more than seventeen years younger than he; a female officer may not marry anyone more than seven years her junior.

In 1966, when U.S. Supreme Court Justice William O. Douglas, then sixty-eight, married twenty-three-year-old Cathy Heffernan, several congressmen called for a full investigation of Douglas's "moral character."

The "experts" are scarcely more free of stereotyped thinking. Take this statement from an anonymous sociologist. The old prejudices are only dressed up here in more sophisticated phrases: "As the man ages, he tends to withdraw, while she is active and vigorous and still wants to go. If he dies, even though they might have been happy, there is the problem of premature widowhood, especially if there were no children. Either the man does not live long, or after a while they find that they do not have much in common. Besides, she has missed the opportunity of dealing with her peers."

The statement smacks of outdated middle-class values: the elderly are useless; pursue security, find friends your own age, and insist on future happiness regardless of what is happening now.

Dr. Benjamin Spock warns visitors that his wife Mary, forty years his junior, believes that "agism is despicable and gets mad when people call attention to our age difference." [2]

Famous sportsman Bud Wilkinson has thirty-three years on his wife, Donna, and she insists, "Age is a non-factor in any person." [3]

Oh well, you may say, these women are married to famous men and are just a bit defensive about it. I doubt it, but listen to what poet-novelist James Dickey, says about his young wife, Deborah. "She can be as rough on a man as a long drunken night in a south Georgia jail—and I love it." [4]

For all the sniggers, however, and in spite of American middle-class myopia, older men in this country have traditionally married much younger women. Until the turn of the century the hazards of childbearing made it common for a man to bury one or two young wives. In the development of the American West, progress was marked by the graves of countless brides.

In more modern times men, for reasons I shall later explore, are generally more attracted to younger women. Today three quarters of all women are younger than their husbands. In a first marriage for both spouses the age difference is usually slight. In

1900, for example, the median marrying ages for women and men were twenty-two and twenty-six. Today it is about twenty-one and twenty-three. In only 8 percent of all first marriages is the bride two or more years older than the groom. Men marrying for a second time, however, tend to marry much younger women: 86 percent of them are older than their new wives—30 percent by ten years or more.[5]

If population trends continue, the number of age-different unions is likely to increase. Barring a large-scale war, major epidemic, or other catastrophe, the over-65 population will grow from an estimated 24 million (or 11 percent of the population) in 1980, to 32 million (about 12 percent) in 2000. We can expect more and more of these people to be attracted to May-December romances.

The signs are everywhere. Songs, novels, movies, and even comic strips use age-different themes. One of the most poignant forms of being secretive about a May-December romance and yet needing to speak out is the anonymous letters appearing in the newspaper columns of by-lined advice-givers. Here's an example of a type that frequently appears.

First, I want you to know that I'm no dummy. I'm a college graduate and have a responsible junior executive position with a large corporation. Ever since high school I've dated men my own age and no matter how carefully I chose them, their immaturity bored me. Long ago I sensed my attraction to older men but thought it unnatural and never acted upon it.

My social life was a mess, and finally I dated an older man whom I'd known and admired for a long time. It was wonderful! I'm so hungry to be held and loved tenderly, and he seemed to understand instantly. He was capable of responding to me on any level, and for the first time in my life I received more from a man than I gave.

I see him and other older men regularly now, but I feel so guilty about it. I don't want my parents to know that I'm "that kind of girl." I try to be very discreet about my older men, but it hurts me to sneak around and be secretive so much. I love my new social life, but feel so horrible and uncertain about what I'm doing, that in a different way I'm in as much trouble as before. Please help me.

Terribly Distressed

The columnist's response to Terribly Distressed was to suggest that she make an appointment with a psychiatrist. In another recent letter a woman complained that although her husband was her age he preferred older women.

I did some checking and learned that when he was in his early twenties he lived with a woman in her forties. Every chance he gets he comes on to older women. I don't know why he married me.

Again, the advice was to try to get her husband to see a psychiatrist. Obviously, columnists who provide advice for the lovelorn are not to be taken as the keepers of society's standards for social behavior. Fortunately, some advice is much more insightful.

Dear Helen,
I'm living proof that age-different marriages work.
When I was 18, I fell in love with 40-year-old Nat. We had 22 terrific married years (two great children) before he died of a sudden heart attack.
We needed each other. Nat almost raised me at first, and I helped him over the middle-age letdown so common to men.
After his death, I discovered my business talents and am now a successful buyer for a large department store.
Now I have met a younger man with whom I feel equal in ambition, potential, and needs. Most people think we're near the same age.
So what if Jim is the step-father of a son only 9 years his junior? They're good pals. My 14-year-old daughter thinks he's great.

Lucky

Dear Lucky,
Thanks for offering more proof that if two people care for one another equally, birth dates aren't important.

P.S. Your life makes a good talking point for those "brave new world" theorists who insist nature stacked the decks.

They point out that females reach their intellectual and physical peak near age 40 while men peak much earlier. So . . . they advocate mid-life divorce for everyone—the 40ish woman finding a younger man who matches her vitality, and her former husband (now in his 60s) finally taking a partner only a few years older than he is (thus "traveling through the twilight years together"). Then when the "young" husband reaches about 45, divorce makes him available for the perpetual youth-middle-age circle. And his wife enters the senior marriage pool.

Another wild projection for the 21st century? Remember, I don't recommend, I only report.

Helen

From Aristotle on, people have been fascinated by the sexual aspect of the May-December romance, and have speculated on it—often with amusing results.[6]

Aristotle, for example, claimed that the ideal marrying age was eighteen for the woman and thirty-seven for the man. He chose these ages so that both partners would experience their sexual decline at roughly the same time—when the man was seventy and the woman fifty. Today Aristotle's opinion would be regarded as poppycock. Research has shown that sexual activities can continue for both men and women until they are near their graves.

In spite of such research, middle-class myth continues to insist that enduring desire is not an attribute of old men. This myth also persists in the face of many interesting historical counterexamples.

In 1583, Thomas Parr, an Englishman, was found guilty of committing adultery at the age of one hundred. He served a sentence according to the custom of the time by wearing a white sheet at the door of the church. To solidify his reputation for all time, Parr remarried at the age of 120 and had children by his second wife.

The Irish poet and playwright, William Butler Yeats, did not marry until he was fifty-two. His book *The Wild Wicked Old Man* was written in his middle seventies and is laced with raw sexuality.

One of my favorite one-liners is the sentence delivered by

Victor Hugo, then eighty-two, to the French Senate. He said, doubtless with a gleam in his eye, "It is difficult for a man of my years to address such an august body—almost as difficult as it is for a man of my years to make love three, no four, times in one afternoon."

For a last bawdy quote, Bernard Berenson, the well-known art historian, confided to his diary shortly before he died at ninety-four, "Only in what might be called my old age have I become aware of sex and the animal in woman."

Words, just words, you may say. It's all in their minds. Consider the story of the ten-year love affair of H. G. Wells and Rebecca West. Wells, for many readers the most exciting writer in English, was forty-five and married when—in 1913—he met West, twenty.

West once remarked to a friend that she would rather have a fifth of a life with Wells than a whole life with anyone. She bore a son during their chaotic romantic affair, and later became a literary figure in her own right.

Once we clear away some of the myths about elderly sex, what can we say about sexual compatibility among May-December couples? Some sociologists say there is more likelihood of serious differences in sexual appetite when there is little age difference than among May-December couples. This speculation hinges, however, on the assumption that sexual activity is less likely to be emphasized by an age-different couple than by coeval couples.

Other sociologists tend to emphasize the sexual motivations of the older husband. He is stereotypically viewed as a man who, fighting clear of a wrecked marriage, seeks a young bride in the hope that she will restore some of his waning sexuality and lost youth. Their studies suggest that his sexual rebirth may be short-lived and that a return to the sexual patterns he had maintained with his coeval wife is likely.

In short, age differences may help sexual compatibility, or hinder it. Or they may have no impact—the experts can't agree.

Other observers suggest that older men are not as likely to be deeply immersed in their careers and are less inclined to become involved with other women.

Friends have speculated that if Charlie Chaplin had married Oona O'Neill when he was thirty or thirty-five, the marriage would not have lasted long. Instead, he married her at fifty-four, when she was eighteen, and the long-term and apparently stable union produced eight children.

Oona has said, "My security and stability with Charlie stemmed from the difference in years between us. Provided that the partners are suited, such a marriage is founded on a rock. The man's character is formed, his life shaped." [7]

The French, those long-time connoisseurs of amorous matters, have a special flair for May-December romances. King Henry II took his father's mistress, Diane de Poitiers, when he was seventeen and she thirty-six. Balzac, the novelist, found his mistress, Madame de Berny, when he was twenty-two and she forty-four, and they were lovers for ten years.

As in so many other romantic matters, a double standard has made it socially less acceptable for an older woman to take up with a younger man. Affairs are more common than marriages.

Sages have extolled the older-woman liaison on the rather obvious grounds that older women are sexually and intellectually more interesting than young women, and in that way offer an invaluable education to a young man. And Stephen Vizinczey in his book *In Praise of Older Women* says that "Boys and girls should leave each other alone. Trying to make love with someone who is unskilled as you seems to be about as sensible as learning to drive with a person who doesn't know the first thing about cars either."

What does May see in December? "A year-round Christmas," replied a wag. And the question of what December sees in May seems never to be asked. The blessings of youthful sex and energy seem all too obvious to answer. In the interviews later in the chapter, May and December speak for themselves. They speak of the strengths, the comforts, and the blessings of their unions. They tell us in clear tones and with obvious joy that May and December can join hands across the generation gap.

First, however, let's read Allen Ginsberg's remarkably elegant statement regarding what May and December harvest and reap.

> . . . that's like an ancient thing and it's very old and charming for older and younger to make it, which you realize as you get old, too—and nothing to be ashamed of, defensive about, but something to be encouraged—a healthy relationship, not a sick neurotic dependency.

The main thing is communication. Older people have ken, experience, history, memory, information, data and also power, money and also worldly technology. Younger people have intelligence, enthusiasm, sexuality, energy, vitality, open mind, athletic activity—all the characteristics and sweet, dewy knowledges of youth; and both profit from the reciprocal exchange. It becomes an exchange of strengths, an exchange of gifts, an exchange of accomplishments, an exchange of nature's bounties. Older people gain vigor, refreshment, vitality, energy, hopefulness and cheerfulness from the attention of the young; and the younger people gain gossip, experience, advice, aid, comfort, wisdom, knowledges and teachings from their relation with the old. So as in other relationships, the combination of old and young is functionally useful. It's far from sexist, in the sense that the interest of the younger person is not totally sexual; it's more in the relationship and the wisdom to be gained.[8]

Ginsberg speaks here of homosexual relationships, but the truth of his comments for all age-different relationships is apparent. Another benefit of the May-December romance is that men who marry young women are generally mature and successful, and these qualities help strengthen a marriage. Humphrey Bogart during his heyday as a film star gained a reputation for candor and succinct statements. When Bogart, at forty-five, married a twenty-year-old Lauren Bacall, he said, "The mature man is more experienced. He has read more books, seen more of the world. He knows how to court a woman. He has learned the hundred little courtesies that make her happy she is a woman." A sexist statement, but Bogart's point is clear.[9]

A twenty-year minimum age difference is used in this book to identify an age-different couple. However, there are so many kinds of age-different couples. If you stop and think about it, a couple aged twenty and forty is likely to be together for different reasons than a forty-sixty couple. And a sixty-eighty couple is probably different from either of those couples. The chronological-age diffrence for the three couples is the same, but their individual levels of personal development and expectations are likely to be very different. Alvin Toffler puts it this way. "Partners will be interested not in age, but in stage."

The timing of the formation of the age-different couples is one way to get a feeling for the nature of some of the May-December romances. Three couples come to mind as examples of the combinations just given.

Bill is a big frog in a little pond. I've know him for years, and he is the first black mayor of the next little town west on the interstate. He's forty-three now, and until nearly two years ago he was single. Indeed, during all those years he was rarely seen in the company of a woman. Bill has always been a writer. Only in recent years has he been able to support himself with his articles, and that was possible only because he became editor of the weekly newspaper in his town. With a steady small income from that part-time job he loves, he can now develop whatever freelance topic pleases him.

It's not always been so good for him. Until his writing income increased he did almost anything he could to keep the writing going. He always told me that he was "a late bloomer."

When he married Julie, twenty-one years his junior and fresh out of school, I went to their wedding. Much later Bill, in his articulate and analytical way, told me about himself in a way he never had.

"It's different for a black man. The reason is basically economic. The less education and income, the more reason to stay single. It took me much longer to achieve the personal and professional maturity and self-awareness that are necessary for a good marriage. Even with my efforts and long delay, I feel like I am barely Julie's emotional equal. And since we're married, it's been my maturity which has been the limiting factor, but I'm learning all the time."

Implicit in Bill's remarks is a message that was to be repeated many times in interviews—it's developmental stage, not chronological age, that counts.

Doctor Joan has helped take care of thousands of babies in her twenty-nine years of work as a pediatrician. Never known by any other name, Dr. Joan looks much younger than sixty-one and she has no children of her own.

When I went to talk to her about her marriage, her opening remark summed up her situation very well. "I buried one husband and wanted another."

Most of her life Joan worked a sixty-hour week. With seemingly infinite energy and obvious relish, she rushed through her life as a doctor and a wife. Married to a mediocre trial lawyer whose efforts to match her personal and professional pace cost him most of his stomach before he was fifty, she never took time to have her own children.

And then when she was sixty, less than a year after her husband died, she married her mailman. That's right. Doctor Joan married her thirty-year-old mailman.

It's a miracle they ever met. Joan was never home when Warner delivered the mail. One day when she was recovering from a brief bout with the flu, Warner found her wrapped in an old bathrobe digging weeds out of her lawn.

Their brief courtship was conducted almost exclusively through hastily scrawled notes left in Joan's mailbox. Joan was instantly taken with Warner's husky outdoorsy appearance, and she freely admits that sex was on her mind from the beginning.

Warner no longer delivers mail. Joan got him involved in managing some of her investments; later he became a real estate agent, and has had minor success as a self-employed businessman.

Joan works less now, and Warner is available to her anytime. They travel a great deal.

Joan and Warner represent another form of age-different coupling. Each had been in a previous marriage. Both were ready for a new life-style. Joan was overworked and Warner wanted freedom. They each got what they wanted from the other. Their relationship is strong and stable.

A few years ago I was taken by a friend to meet Larry. I'd never have found him by myself. He lives in a remote mountainous area up a long dirt road which has a locked gate where it joins the main highway. Larry is an artist and has a modest regional reputation. He is eighty-three and has lived for over sixty years in the house he built with his own hands.

"The house is a memorial to Larry's life. It is rambling, with many wings and outlying cabins; each was built as a part of some phase of his life.

There is a small central section, just a big bookcase-lined room with a fireplace, where Larry lived as a young single man. He drifted into painting as a means of supporting himself when his savings ran out, and a bright, airy studio was added to the north.

His first wife was a writer, and she chose a small sunny meadow at the end of a footpath running northwest from the house as the site of her writing cabin. Larry also added a bedroom to the south.

Larry's first marriage lasted over twenty years and along the way a modern kitchen and bathroom were joined to the core structure.

Larry's first wife died in her mid-fifties, and he won't discuss it. I sense a deep and continuing sorrow.

The second important woman in his life formed a May-December romance. He had lived as a widower for over two years when late on a wet spring afternoon Anne appeared at his door and announced that she wanted to work with him.

Anne was in her mid-twenties, more than thirty years younger than Larry, and had just graduated from art school. She moved into Larry's quiet life like a whirling dervish.

At first she stayed in the writing cabin, but soon she was sharing Larry's bed, and then he built her a studio attached to his. Larry once pointed out to me that the two studios were carefully arranged so that Larry and Anne could see each other through a doorway while they were working.

Anne was not a gifted artist, but she developed a clever etching technique which caught on, and she was able to sell most of her work.

I don't know why Anne stayed so long. The solitude of the setting was hard on her. There were troubles with drinking, and occasionally she would leave for several days without saying a word. One day, after nearly ten years, she left and never came back.

Larry married a second time a few years ago when he was eighty. If you visit him today, you will see a second bedroom and two small guest cottages not far from the main house. Larry admits with a smile that he has had "lots of young help" on his construction projects in recent years.

Sylvia is nineteen years younger than Larry, a widow with

grown children and grandchildren, and she lives most of the time in her large house in a nearby town.

Larry is comfortable and happy in the woods, and Sylvia likes town life. They visit each other, spend weekends together, take trips abroad, and entertain dozens of Sylvia's relatives at Larry's hideaway. They share a deep interest in art and music.

They get exactly what they want from each other. Larry says they married in deference to Sylvia's family and because "we're straight."

Larry and Sylvia represent a third kind of age-different union. I call it a "September Song Marriage." Money and sex are not serious concerns, but the partners reach across the generation gap to meet those needs which seem harder to achieve because of aging—companionship, interest, loyalty, and shared activities. By the time people are eighty-three and sixty-four, as are Larry and Sylvia, the generation gap has, for all practical purposes, disappeared.

Our culture's traditional marriage formula assumes that two young people will find each other, marry, fulfill a variety of needs for one another, and develop over the years more or less in tandem "until death do us part."

The basic stimulus is always love, and this particular kind of love uses a mesh of complementary emotional needs to produce feelings of warmth, tenderness, and devotion. Marriage partners who stay together "grow together" in love, and the social, educational, or intellectual development is left to good luck. The odds against this parallel development are enormous—as mounting divorce rates demonstrate. With too great a discrepancy in developmental stages, couples may call it quits. Now more people instinctively use developmental state as a basis for mate selection—and the age-different couple is a natural consequence.

Bill and Julie, the first couple described earlier, have a May-December marriage which was formed because of Bill's delayed emotional growth. It's not that simple; however, they appear to have matched similar emotional stages in a mutually satisfying way.

Joan and Warner matched different, but complementary, stages.

As a couple they have a perfection of life that neither could achieve alone.

Larry and Sylvia are at similar developmental stages even though their age gap is nineteen years. They appear to be rather different people who, nevertheless, share common needs. Their attitudes and expectations allow satisfying those needs together with a minimum of difficulty.

When we studied mathematics in school we learned that there were basic laws upon which everything was built. These axioms are unshakable truths from which all arithmetic operations flow, and you don't change them in order to solve a problem. Love relations in our culture seem constituted in a similar way. Many parents must have been through the following dialogue with sons or daughters when informed of an engagement.

> Parent: But what do you see in him (her)?
> Answer: I love him (her)!

There it is—the unimpeachable principle upon which most middle-class matings are based.

If the parents are being informed that their son is establishing a permanent liaison with a woman thirty-five years his senior, they might wonder if he's mentally defective, but they are more likely to discredit the utility of such a union, than seriously examine the sanity of the participants. All the cliches about May-December romances are trotted out and put on display. It's made clear that the partners are deceiving themselves and that the relationship can't last.

Implicit in the societal resistance is the judgment that age-different partners are out of touch with their feelings, needs, and foibles. I disagree.

But what if I really am looking for a father figure or trying to recapture my lost youth? Should I accept a societal stigma that labels me immature, especially when I am happy and content with my life? And if my relationship doesn't make me happy next year, no one is going to delude me into thinking that I wasn't happy this year.

These issues are at the foundation of all human interactions and our expectations of what those interactions should be. It is a fact of life that there is pain associated with living. Society and its representatives, professions, often "medicalize" the pain of living. By doing this, society promotes avoidance of certain life-styles or suggests counseling to facilitate a change to more acceptable forms. The choice, however, is ours.

The May-December romance challenges the traditional qualifications for a cohabiting contract made for an exchange of need gratifications. We must question the limitations on the qualifications and the gratifications.

There is no flaw in May-December romances that should persuade anyone to avoid them. Indeed, in many instances the attitudes, needs, stages, and goals of a particular individual suggest that an age-different relationship may be more suitable than a coeval one. To discredit the possibility of such a union because of a stigma or for any other reason is to lose a rich alternative and thereby limit your life options.

CHAPTER TWO

A Priceless Treasure

IT WAS MIDDAY when Jesalee and I drove into the foothills. The Sierra Nevadas formed a striking background for the rolling oak-studded hills at their base. Tucked in a small grassy valley we found the house where Lou and Ed live.

I was nervous. When the house finally appeared at the end of the winding dirt road we were following, my foot instinctively released the gas pedal as though to delay our arrival.

I'm rarely comfortable interviewing age-different couples, even under the "safest" circumstances. Probing into the personal life of strangers makes my stomach churn. Our questions often prompt one of the couple to relate stories or experiences that come as a surprise to the other. Those moments of discovery can be awkward, especially when the tales of a former lover are told.

But the most difficult moment is when I lean forward and with a straining voice say, "My readers are going to want to know about your sex life." There follows an indescribable pause while we wait to see who will start talking and about what.

Today though, the tension was already high, for this was no "safe" interview coming up. Ed and Lou differed in age by forty years—he was seventy-two, she thirty-two. Tangled up in my usual nervousness were memories of old Mr. Macintosh, and some of the past confusion and fear gnawed at me.╱

As Jes and I climbed the steps to the porch, the front door was pushed open and Lou and Ed stepped out. They stood hip to hip waiting for us. We walked to them and much of my nervousness washed away. In that moment of meeting an immediate sense of trust passed between us. That feeling is with me today.

Lou and Ed are cast from the same mold. Both are short and thickish—Lou in the hips and Ed in the belly. They wore western work clothes and their boots were muddy. Both have round faces, and Ed's smile was broad while Lou's was shy.

Lou took Jes's arm and led her inside, but Ed clapped his hands on my shoulders and stood with his eyes locked on mine. After a moment he said, "We've been waiting for you, and while we were waiting something that happened to me when I was a young fellow kept running through my mind. Before we do anything, I want to tell you that story." That story was my first glimpse of the seasoned common sense that Ed brings to his life. I want you to meet him in the same way.

When I was a young kid, I spent some time cowboying in Nevada. We'd catch a few head of wild horses and take them to the railroad in Winnemuca for shipment. I never really knew where those mustangs wound up—I heard a dog food factory in California. After the horses were loaded there was nothing else to do so we'd head for the local saloon. They were all the same in those days—a few card tables and a bar downstairs, and the whores waiting in their rooms upstairs.

The old guys in our crew were fatherly to me. They'd sit me down with a sarsaparilla, then get drunk and whoop it up with the women. We all carried six-shooters. You never knew when a horse might break his leg or there'd be a rattlesnake or a rabid coyote. Once in a while you might want to scare somebody.

One day a bunch of Idaho cowboys came in with some wild horses, and they were wearing guns and shooting some. Later one of them got a little drunk and said he was going to shoot out the lights in the saloon.

As he was popping the bulbs, one of his shots went wild and hit a young prostitute. We found out later that the bullet passed inside her arm, just creasing her ribs.

She hit the floor screaming that she was shot and dying. Lying there squirming in the crap and sawdust, she moaned, "Don't let me die in a place like this."

We carried her outside and laid her on the gravel road and they sent me for the doctor. I ran all around town before I found him drinking in another saloon, and when I told him what had happened he said, "Don't worry about Elva, she won't die." He was drunk anyway.

I was pooped from running after the doctor, then Elva insisted I get the minister. Taking off like some old horse blown out after chasing mustangs, I found the minister and he gave Elva the last rites.

When the minister was finished Elva looked up and said, "I ought to be married 'fore I die."

At that point an old fart of a cowboy, must have been over eighty, who was always hanging around the saloon stepped forward and said, "I ain't doing nothing—I'll marry you."

The old timer figured she was going to die, but after the minister had married the drunk and the prostitute right there in the street, Elva immediately began to get better. She started spouting about curtains and dishes and all that stuff.

And do you know—about a year or so later when we were back in town on a cattle drive, there's Elva and the old cowboy happy as two peas in a pod. She was especially nice to us because we had "attended her wedding." She served up a special dinner—even put napkins on the table. While we were eating, one of my buddies said, "Elva, I heard of lots of different ways of catching a man, but you sure went all out on this one."

Elva smiled a smile I didn't know she had in her and answered, "I could of done it differently, and done a lot worse."

Lou and Ed married nearly two years ago—lived together for a year before that. I sat, still chuckling over Ed's story, at the kitchen table in their small ranch house. Living room and kitchen were one large space—paintings on the wall, books everywhere, and a few pieces of worn furniture. A stack of dishes perched on the drain board, and something in the oven smelled good.

An elderly red setter sprawled asleep in the middle of the room. A few moments after we sat down the aroma of baking gave way to a pungent stench that wrinkled my nostrils and stopped all breathing for a moment. "Don't worry," Ed said looking at the dog, "Beauregard's got some gas."

When we talk to age-different couples we almost always begin by asking about their parents. This is a comfortable topic and most people enjoy talking about their childhood. For nearly an hour we listened to stories about the remarkable fathers of Lou and Ed. It became clear to us that both their fathers shaped Lou and Ed in significant ways. To help know more about Lou and Ed, let's take a brief look at their parents' background.

Ed's father, Pedro, was born in Spain in 1858. Both of Pedro's sisters were nuns and his brother was a priest, but Pedro took a different path. He went to an academy of science and graduated as a mining engineer, chemist, and druggist.

Always restless and never comfortable in the family life, Pedro came to this country in the early 1890s and operated a drugstore in Idaho. He became a U.S. citizen, but during the Spanish-American War his neighbors harassed him, and after stones were thrown through his drugstore window he decided to go to Mexico for a while.

In Mexico, Pedro was the superintendent of a copper mine and known locally as "the Spanish Dandy." He was a fancy dresser, and when he came to town he wore beaded buckskin chaps and rode a white mule.

Dorthea Emmett was a proper San Francisco lady of Scottish and English heritage. The daughter of the owner of one of the first newspapers in San Francisco, she was educated in a private college and became a schoolteacher.

On a visit to a wealthy Mexican family with her sisters and mother, Dorthea met Pedro. After a short romantic courtship that startled her family, Dorthea, twenty-five, married Pedro, fifty, and startled them even more.

Ed, one of five boys, was born in Mexico in 1905, arrived in San Francisco the day before the city was devastated by earthquake, and spent his youth there.

The year after Ed's birth, Theodore Walk was born in a small town near Boston. A short man of Ukrainian background, he left school after the eighth grade and worked as a shoe salesman for four years. Sensing the dead-end street he was on, Theodore returned to Boston and supported himself through high school. Then, still paying his own way, he earned a degree from Harvard. Boston University was next and he graduated from its school of medicine as a physician. Theodore was the classic case of the hometown boy who made good in spite of family poverty and national depression.

Theodore returned to develop a medical practice in Newton, near where he was raised, and married the woman he had been seeing for seven years. Lou was born in 1945.

Theodore's practice in Newton was interrupted by two wars— World War II and Korea—in both of which he served as an army medical officer. Rather than try to set up his private practice for the third time, Theodore decided to remain in the army. Lou was raised in a series of exotic but safe army posts settings where her father was stationed.

As our talk progressed I learned several facts about Lou's life. Always attracted to medical activities, she had been involved in nursing since her late teens—first as an aide, then up the ladder to a degree and registration. Now she taught nursing courses at a community college not far from the ranch.

I also learned that Lou had been married previously. When I inquired about her first husband, her body stiffened; and her face went blank. Sitting erect in her chair, she delivered the story of her first marriage in a dull monotone.

I was such a different person when I was with my first husband. He was an honorable man and I loved him, but it seemed like I was his mother and raising him. I had to teach him that hot stoves burn and barbed wire scratches and after nearly seven years I got tired of it. He was an honest, hard-working, struggling young man when we married, and though superficially we had all the ingredients for a successful marriage, there was no deep meaning to our relationship. It was so difficult for him to show his feelings for me.

Whenever I did something which I felt was creative, he would scorn it. Finally I did drawings in secret and hid them. He would tease me about my nose and call me funny names. I got tired of being put down.

Through most of our marriage we both worked full time, but I had the total responsibility for the house and for our daughter. I told him he should hire a housekeeper, a laundress, a cook, and he could even have a mistress for all we had in the marriage. He would be getting the same thing with either arrangement.

At last I got out of my unworthiness enough to realize it was okay for me to have a way and to seek it, and I left.

He's good to our daughter now and from my freedom I can better accept him the way he is.

Ed broke in at this point to say, "Lou's ex-husband has a veiled eye—looks at you with something hidden. He's the kind of person who never really lets you into his life."

I sensed a deep uneasiness in Lou during her story. Ed, apparently sensitive to her, remained quietly in the background until she had finished. Usually there was an ongoing banter between the two, and Lou loosened up the most during those moments.

Ed is like a bouncing ball. He's full of energy, and with only slight encouragement he will bounce over and tell a story. A compulsive talker, he has a rich background to tap. He has been a boxer, rodeo rider, rancher, and owner and trainer of race horses. From his many tales I was able to piece together some of his history.

Educated in western schools, Ed won many titles in collegiate and amateur boxing on the Pacific Coast, capping them all with the national collegiate championship in his division. He boxed professionally for three years, then bought a ranch and became involved in breeding and training race horses. Recently he has written books and songs and sold paintings.

Ed's previous marriage lasted thirty-five years. He was widowed in 1969 when his wife died of cancer. I asked him about his first marriage.

I think of myself as a kind of bum. I like to live rough, work hard, and keep my life as simple as it can be. Let me work outside with animals, and with ordinary bed and board, that's all I need. I can get along with anyone—especially if I'm determined. My first wife wanted to live fancy and raise race horses so that's what we did. But there were lots of times I felt like rolling my bed and getting out.

I always felt that I owed the world something—that I should be raising food or helping people. Raising race horses is the toughest racket in the world, but I was consoled by the idea that horse racing was helping agriculture. County fairs, agricultural schools, and all the young farmer organizations like 4-H receive lots of support from horse racing.

I feel everything, and I'm so deeply grateful for being alive in all the beauty we have around us. I don't mean it's peaches and cream. Things happen. I love animals but a mule kicked me in the mouth once and knocked all my teeth out. Another time a horse fell on me and smashed my hip. Now I can never get on an airplane without my steel hip setting off the alarm at the gate.

I asked Ed about his life after he was widowed.

That was strange. I was free, but I wasn't free. I had the entire ranch to handle, and I just didn't go anyplace. My friends figured I was holed up and hurting. After I hadn't been seen for a long time, my racetrack buddies came up with the idea that I was mentally disturbed so they sent a psychiatrist up to see me. One morning he pulled up to the ranch in his big car. I'd had a bad night—been up with a mare that had foaled and I was watching an old cow about to have a calf. I hadn't shaved and I was a mess. I was stirring a big pot of beans on the stove when the psychiatrist walked up. He said, "I'm Doctor so-and-so."

I said "Good morning, Doc, there's nothing wrong with the horses—everything is all right."

"Well," the doctor said, "I'm not a veterinarian. Your friends sent me up here to evaluate your mental condition."

I said, "Doc, I'm too damned busy to have a mental condition."

The doctor insisted on talking to me—said my friends were worried about me, so I took him in the barn and we sat on a bale of hay near that mare I was keeping an eye on. For a while the doctor watched me run between the mare and the cow, stir the beans and kick a dog in the ass after he grabbed a chicken. Finally the doctor said, "You need some female company."

I answered, "Doc, do you know a good woman who can wash, cook, and sew, and take care of the ranch? Until she comes along, every couple of weeks I visit a place where the women probably don't have degrees, but they sure give relief and it's worth the money."

With that the doc just about fell off that bale of hay, but he laughed and told me how concerned my friends at the track were about me. He had a bowl of beans with me and went on to say how he envied my ranch life and how he wished he had friends as strong and caring as mine.

I've introduced you to Ed and Lou and you know something about their background. It's time for their meeting. Picture the scene. Ed is a crusty rancher, widowed now for six years, nearly seventy years old and making do. Lou is not yet thirty, divorced six months, sharing a small house with a woman friend and teaching at a community college. They live a few miles apart, but have never met.

On weekend evenings Ed sometimes goes to a small town bar called the Oak Grill (I'd call it a roadhouse and Lou claims it's a dive). One evening after much pressure from her housemate, Lou sat in the dimness having a drink. She described meeting Ed in this way: "I'm very nearsighted and the Oak was like a black pit, when suddenly a man in a big cowboy hat appeared next to our table. He tipped his hat and asked if I wanted to dance. I said that I didn't know, so he thanked me and went away. The owner of the bar had seen me turn Ed away, so he came over and told me Ed was okay. A few minutes later I was dancing with Ed. And there it was!"

QUESTION: Did the two of you hit it off that night?

LOU: No—well, we kinda did. He was so easy to talk to and so gentlemanly.

QUESTION: What was your reaction when you realized he was a much older man?

LOU: Every now and then it would hit me, but I was always able to pass it up because of the person he is. When I thought about it intellectually, I realized it didn't make any difference because of the quality of the interaction we were having. That outweighed everything. [*Lou sounds as if she is lecturing.*]

QUESTION: When did you learn Ed's age?

LOU: Almost immediately he told me, and later when I knew we were getting together I thought—he's almost seventy, and this can't last forever. Then an inner voice answered my own thoughts saying—You chump, this happiness is being offered to you right now. Are you going to let it go because it isn't going to last for a hundred years? [*Delivered with firmness.*]

QUESTION: How much time do you want, Lou?

LOU: I want Ed to live at least till ninety when I'll be fifty. I'll settle for that. [*Soft and contemplative here.*]

QUESTION: What is it that's so special about Ed?

LOU: I appreciate having a man like Ed not only because of his age, but because of the kind of person he is and has always been. He loves me for what I am, and he treats me like a priceless treasure always. There is no competition between us. If he does well at something I'm joyful about it. If I do well at something, he's joyful about it. And this reinspires each of us to do more and more. He's not interested in my body all the time, which I terribly resented before. Ed is able to recognize and appreciate my inner qualities, and I think it takes a wise older man to do that. I'm convinced that if you listen to your own intuition and inner urging, you'll know what's right for you and then you must be willing to accept it when it does come. That's what I did.

Lou answered my questions as if she were playing an internal tape recorder—no spontaneity at all. Every remark seemed carefully thought out in advance. I suspect she has answered similar questions many times.

These were questions we asked Ed:

QUESTION: What were your relationships with women after you were widowed and before you met Lou?

ED: All kinds of widows found ways to meet me. Some had been married to old friends of mine who had died. Most of them put me off. All they talked about were hats, food, houses, and the latest movie. I'm interested in deeper things.

QUESTION: Surely you met other types of women nearer your age?

ED: Sure, let me tell you about one. I knew her husband well before he died. She had a big ranch, oil holdings, but she wanted to run everything, including me. When she talked about marriage I looked the deal over and said, "What the hell, play second fiddle again, I'm free now—I don't want any of this."

QUESTION: How do you get along with Lou's eight-year-old daughter?

ED: We've had some tough times. I get up in the middle of the night, take her to the bathroom and drain her. She'd purposely lie in bed and wet—wouldn't get up. Now she's starting to do it by herself. Kids are tougher to raise than horses, 'cause they're smarter. I'm developing a strong feeling for her and she is for me. We have a lot of respect for each other. [*Very subdued and serious.*]

QUESTION: Do people ever mistake Lou for your daughter?

ED: Sure, all the time. They say to me—I saw your daughter— and I reply—Yeah, nice looking girl, isn't she. [*Laughing.*]

QUESTION: Seriously, Ed, do you run into any problems when you and Lou go out socially?

ED: Only from those widows that used to chase me. They seem to resent her. It used to bother Lou some, but I believe that if you know what you can do, who you are, and what you want, you don't have to depend on anyone else.

QUESTION: Ed, what is your reaction to having a young wife?

ED: She comes up to me and pats me and says you got to keep that hair and she likes me, and I feel just like an old saddle horse. I've had 'em; they were old, but they always got the job done. Nothing about being married to Lou ever offends me.

QUESTION: Don't old saddle horses need a lot of extra care?

ED: No, I'm more worried about her. She's getting heavy 'cause she eats too much, she's smoking, and she's got bad feet. If she gets too much weight, she's going to break down. What am I going to do with a big fat broke-down woman—I'll have to push her around in a wheelchair. [*Lou laughs, runs to Ed and cuffs him.*]

QUESTION: You referred to Lou as your project. What does that mean?

ED: I teach her a lot—especially about financial things and future security. I do everything I can to help her build a foundation for the long life she has ahead of her. [*Preachy.*]

QUESTION: Do you ever worry about getting old and weak and becoming dependent on Lou?

ED: I'll never be dependent on anyone. When I get so I can't take care of myself anymore, I'm going to a spot I know in Nevada. The old Indians used to sit there. I'll wear an arctic suit, and take wine, bread, and cheese with me. I'll have a little party with myself, be happy, then I'll open the zipper and let Jack Frost come in. [*Completely comfortable talking about this.*]

[*Lou breaks in.*] I think a great deal about what Ed is saying. It is his life and his choice. My choice is to accept what is here for us now, and to be able to let go when it's time to let go. I don't think it would be a loving act if I tried to force Ed to be in a hospital or a nursing home. I know he doesn't want that. [*Lou is very intense.*]

ED: My deepest concern in marrying Lou was that I was being unfair to her. I believed I was being selfish to impose my life on hers.

QUESTION: Why did you get married? Why not just live together?

ED: She proposed. [*Lou is sputtering.*] I had it in my mind all the time, but she proposed. When we were living together I noticed a few raised eyebrows, particularly in my set—the old-fashioned narrow-minded ones.

[*Lou breaks in.*] With the living-together arrangement, until marriage occurs, the total commitment is not there. One must keep part of oneself in reserve just in case. Now we can build and plan. Only now in my mind can I establish a sense of permanence to our tie. Call it old-fashioned or whatever, but for me emotionally it made a big difference.

ED: And it has for me, too. I felt guilty when we were living together. The way I was raised—it just didn't set right with me.

LOU: For me our marriage formed a spiritual bond. Before the wedding, in our hearts, we felt married. But now it's stronger, as though some subtle ingredient has been added.

In our marriage we cooperate to get any job done. Ed does everything here to help out. He cleans, gets my daughter up and off to school, does any chore and is a great cook.

ED: The other day some of my old cronies were joshing me about washing the dishes and I came right back—Yeah, I got it good. Before Lou I used to do the cooking *and* wash the dishes.

LOU [*laughing*]: He gives people all kinds of different answers about his house chores. Sometimes when he's kidded about his dishwashing he says—Yeah, I might want to pee in the sink and I can't do it if it's full of dirty dishes.

[*Lou turns serious.*]

In our kind of marriage it's crystal clear that you haven't got time for the petty crap. You know it isn't going to last forever so all of your effort goes toward getting along, taking happiness while you can take it, and making more happiness 'cause it doesn't drop in your lap. The age difference makes us truly appreciate what's here right now.

I want to tell you about something else. All my life I've had creative desire—not much ability but lots of desire. My education was academic, and in my first marriage the inspiration wasn't there. One of the most beautiful aspects of our relationship is the creative flow that we allow and foster in each other. Often we don't clean for weeks but Ed paints and writes constantly and I sew and paint when I can. We never worry about how our place looks when people come to visit.

ED: We live—we enjoy life—we aren't slaves to anyone.

LOU: We decided a long time ago that there will be no third party of any kind allowed to interfere with our relationship—no relative, friend, institution, idea, or religion can come between us. What we have is sacred, and from it we give out good energy which everyone can share.

QUESTION: What is your sex life like? [*Both tighten a little.*]

LOU: In my first marriage the only time I got any affection was during sex. I was burned by that experience. In thinking back I realize he was a very physical person and I'm not. With Ed, our physical life is so different. We embrace frequently, we kiss when we pass each other, and when we have sex it's just great.

ED: You can learn a lot about sex by watching the animals. There are certain times in an animal's cycle when they demand sex. I've seen an old cow run up and down the fence—bawling and yelling—trying to attract the neighbor's bull. That's the time to have sex. If you're going to promote sex when the woman isn't interested, it isn't very enjoyable.

LOU: Our sexual relationship is very satisfactory.

ED [*with emphasis*]: Very satisfactory.

LOU: Ed treats me like a priceless treasure in sex just as he does in all our interactions.

ED: I respect her. It's something that's sacred in married life. Something that should never be mentioned casually. When I hear one of my friends say, "Well, I tore off a piece last night —the old lady was never better," I turn away.

LOU: Knowing that Ed feels that way increases my admiration for him a thousandfold. Anything that is private to us will never be discussed openly. Our sex life does not play a major role in our total life. It's there in its rightful place.

ED: Sexual activity cannot play a major role and last. I've seen it time and time again. Some guy says, "I'm going to marry this gal—man, what she can do in bed." There's a lack of respect before the marriage, and the marriage doesn't last.

LOU: The first time Ed meets a woman, he treats her as a lovely woman. He does not automatically think of her in a sexual way. This is why women are drawn to Ed. They know that implicit respect and strong true friendships are possible with him. [*Firmly.*]

ED [*speaking to Jesalee*]: I talk to you; I admire you as a person; we're equal. There's no barrier because you're a woman and I'm a man. I'm not going to step over the line, we're both on the same line.

Ed told me about his brother, Jim.

ED: Jim is seventy-three. He supports his wife in a nursing home because she is very senile and can't take care of herself. Now he has a lady friend and we welcome them in our home. Jim is vital and living alone, she is a widow living alone, and what the hell are two old people gonna do to get in trouble. I think it's wonderful. Life is happiness right now. Not promises of tomorrow or of the great beyond when you die. It's right here and right now.

QUESTION: Any last comments about age-different relationships?

ED: Being an old horse trader, I'd never buy an old horse when I could get a young one. [*Big laugh.*]

LOU: I don't think I sought Ed as a replacement-father figure, but I loved and admired my father so much, that I wanted to marry a man like him. I did not actively seek an older man, but I was always drawn to older men, in preference to younger men, because they displayed more of these qualities. [*Another tape.*]

ED: I wouldn't trade Lou for one of those new coal oil stoves with three burners and an oven. [*The room fills with laughter.*]

The time spent with Lou and Ed was special. Their warmth and openness allowed immediate friendship, and we are friends today. Before we left their home Ed told me of a prayer he wrote and recites each night before sleep.

Let there be peace on earth with all men free. With schools, churches, and hospitals within reach of every soul on this earth. Let us use atomic power to reclaim the jungles, to clear the brush land, to drain the swamps, and to water the wasteland. To plant, produce, process, and transport food wherever there is hunger. Let all of our children grow up together regardless of race, creed, or color with equal opportunity in their environment to become happy, healthy, useful, friendly citizens of the world with peace foremost in mind. Thank you, Lord, for another day and all the beauty you've given us to enjoy. And thank you, Lord, for Lou. And thank you for burnt umber and dark sienna.

Lou and Ed are living testimony that an age-different couple can tolerate a host of pressures and thrive. They exude appreciation for each other—not for a romantic ideal, but for themselves.

In some ways Lou and Ed seem too well adjusted. Their doubts, fears, and questions have been dealt with, and the quick answers are all figured out. That isn't true, of course; not any more for them than for anyone else. The anxiousness surfaces now and then. But they are in this world, living richly and surviving well, and I applaud them.

CHAPTER THREE

Let's
Not Reinvent
the Wheel

VIRTUALLY ALL SOCIETIES have advocated marriage as the most desirable type of existence for adults. Marriage usually meant living together, working together, having children, and raising them.

Mate selection has never been a random activity. Two features of selection work together to choose that special person. First, cultural traditions and customs create a field of eligible prospects into which a person is encouraged to marry. And second, several people, including the participants, are involved in varying degrees in making the final selection. This has been the rule of marriage in every known human group, past or present, primitive or modern.

In America, Jim Smith marries Jane Greene because he loves her. In feudal Japan, Ito Satake took Haru Taira as his wife because their families arranged it. Among the Yaruro Indians of Venezuela, José Miguel wed Anita because she was his mother's brother's daughter. Gogab Garub, a Hottentot man in Southwest Africa, could not marry the woman he wanted because she was his seventh cousin; instead, he married Hoaras Garis, who met the stringent kinship requirements of the Hottentots. In all four of these marriages, the ages of the partners differ by fifteen to twenty years.

The Jim Smiths and Jane Greenes of America are the subject of this book. They are challenging the customary narrowing of their field of eligible mates. It doesn't take much study to reveal that in many cultures at various times, conditions have acted to produce age-different marriages. The reasons may have been social, economic, or religious. Exploring the lives of the three couples just mentioned, and other historical versions of marriages, will help establish our cultural legacy and assist in understanding age-different relationships of today.

In Japan of the 1700s, arranged marriage was found in its purest form. Social classes were defined rigidly, and family life was organized around the patriarch. He ruled over his wife, all his sons and their wives and children, his unmarried daughters, servants, and younger brothers of the patriarch and their wives and children. Marriage decisions, however, were usually made by the mature males and the old women of the family functioning as a council.

Children were raised in a setting with rigid expectations and almost ritual performance of even the simplest tasks. The continual threat of humiliation or withdrawal of family affection forced the children's submission. They learned to think not as individuals, but as family members. By adulthood, all family interaction was based on kinship, not personal feelings.

Marriage was an affair of the entire family. People married to keep the family going, and that concern governed the choice of mate. Marriage was so important to all members of both families that neither the participants nor the patriarch were trusted with the arrangements. The family council considered first the social class, honor, and health of the members of the proposed family. With these conditions met, only secondarily were the mates identified. With such a miniscule field of choice, age-different partners were common.

Neither Ito Satake nor Haru Taira had any voice in the arrangements, and in fact did not meet until the wedding ceremony.

The families were being united, and individual qualities meant little.

Family intervention in mate selection was even more involved in other settings.[1] In India the combination of religious prohibition of remarriage for women, but not for men, and the religious emphasis on children (and high mortality of women in childbirth) produced great interest in marriage but poor balance between marriageable males and females. Family-arranged child brides were the consequence. A recent census in India listed nearly half a million widows under the age of fifteen.

Fathers arranged marriages for their children as early as age seven. Virginity was considered essential for the bride, and the best way to ensure this state was to marry her off as soon as possible after the initial menstruation. The male could be of any age, though he was usually around twenty.

The fall of the Roman Empire brought chaos and many changes to Western Europe. During the early Middle Ages, roving bands alternated between fighting each other and attacking villages. Child marriages were common. In those troubled times, parents used their children to establish beneficial defensive, political, or economic alliances. It was easier to manipulate children when they were very young. The age of seven was considered the age of reason; however, some of the partners were even younger. These political and economic conditons of the Middle Ages caused many of the marriages to be age-different.

The church of that period pleaded that no babies in the crib should be married "unless there was some pressing need." Marriage between children could be dissolved if it had not been consummated. The rule of thumb: If the boy was more than fourteen and the girl more than twelve, intercourse was assumed if they had been to bed.

The most famous love affair of the Middle Ages was an age-different relationship. Abelard was thirty-eight years old in 1118, and a famous scholar of theology and philosophy. He was a canon of the Cathedral of Notre Dame. Weary of chastity, he moved into the home of another canon, Fulbert, in order to meet Fulbert's niece, Heloise. Abelard was an arrogant, egotistical man whose theological successes paradoxically convinced him that he no longer had to deny himself earthly pleasures.

He sought Heloise, then eighteen, because she was beautiful, brilliant, and educated. Abelard's chastity soon ended, but by the time Fulbert became aware of it and sent him away, Heloise was pregnant.

Part of this couple's fame stems from the discovery of their love letters and the intimate window to their affair the letters offered. Ultimately, Abelard was castrated by agents of Fulbert and became a monk. Heloise took the nun's veil and was very successful in the convent.

During the Renaissance the minimum marriageable age was about twelve for girls. The practice of oldsters marrying youngsters for special benefit continued, although two pressures developed to end child marriages. It was generally believed that sperm was essential for proper mental and physical growth, and none should be wasted prematurely. In addition, a girl who gave birth before she was sixteen threatened the health of both herself and the infant.

Perhaps the most extreme case of parental intervention in the mate-selection of their offspring was among the Kazaks of central Asia. It was not uncommon for Kazak fathers to make binding marriage agreements for children not yet born.[2]

Kinship requirements are the second major basis of mate-selection. Recall that José Miguel married Anita because she was his mother's brother's daughter. They are members of the Yaruros, a tribe of river nomads who live on the plain southeast of the Andes in inland Venezuela. The Yaruros live a simple life based on hunting and fishing. They live on the river, migrate in canoes, and own almost nothing. A riverside camp of Yaruros is likely to include an old man and his wife, their unmarried sons and daughters, their married daughters and husbands, their grandchildren, and sometimes unmarried brothers and sisters.

Yaruro society is divided into moieties or halves on the basis of kinship. One inherits his moiety from his mother, and must marry into the opposite moiety. Therefore, a Yaruro man must marry one of his mother's brothers' daughters, or one of his father's sisters' daughters—a cross-cousin.

Their fragile nomadic life suggests that the Yaruros might favor close kinship marriages; however, they consider it incest for a male to marry his sisters, his mother, his mother's sisters' daughters, and his father's brothers' daughters. That leaves only cross-cousins, and this excessive narrowing of the choices means that age makes absolutely no difference.

The selection procedure has a very practical foundation. In a land where there is poor communication and sparse population, a mate can be found nearby, but the individual must be from another camp. Interaction between camps is promoted, and interfamilial solidarity is maintained in that harsh land.

As if all this weren't enough, the choice of cross-cousin must be made by the uncle of the boy—who is also the father of the girl.

Spouses chosen by kinship requirements have been the rule in many settings. The Bible is our chief source of information about the ancient Hebrews. They were a mobile people who were forever at war. Few infants survived such danger and upheaval, so the culture emphasized children. Everyone was expected to marry at an early age, even priests. Marriage between family members was favored: Abraham married a half sister; his bother Nahor married a niece; and Amram, the father of Moses, wed his aunt. With only relatives to choose from, age-different matches were a natural consequence. As the Hebrews settled into a patriarchal culture and practiced farming, restrictions were placed on maternal half-sister marriages.

As mentioned earlier, Gogab Barub, a Hottentot man, could not marry Hoaras Baris because she was his seventh cousin. The Hottentots practice a reverse-kinship requirement for marriage. This nomadic tribe herds cattle and sheep and hunts on grassy plateaus in the southwestern corner of Africa. Women work hard, and the men are generally lazy. After boys and girls have passed a series of puberty rites, they are allowed a great deal of sexual freedom, and are restricted little in the choice of a mate. The major selection limitation prohibits marrying a person with whom a common ancestor is shared.

The young man must go to a nearby camp to locate a marriageable woman. Both bride and groom have a voice in the arrangements, and because the choices may be severely limited, age-different couples are common.

Beyond family-arranged marriages and unions based on kinship rules, a variety of economic concerns and customs of obscure origin create age-different unions. In rural China of a few decades ago, elder women were preferred to younger as wives, because they were better workers. During the same period, a more enlightened young Chinese woman in a city sought a husband twice her age plus one year.

In primitive Brazilian tribes, there were many uncle-niece and aunt-nephew marriages, because of a custom which gave older people prior claim on the young. Young Australian tribesmen did not marry until age thirty, and then they wed widows and old women. In the same tribe, widowed older men of forty-five and fifty married young girls of ten and twelve who had been betrothed to them in infancy. No amount of study has revealed the basis for these customs.

My research turned up an old saying which specified that a woman should marry a man twice her age less seven years. This old rule was especially interesting, because it gives the age conditions under which I married my wife Jesalee.

The early Greeks regarded age-similar marriages as unnatural. They preferred the male older by ten to fifteen years when he married at about thirty-five. They did not favor the marriage of young men, and frowned when people beyond their reproductive years wed those in their fruitful years.

The golden age of Greece was recorded in enough detail in the period between the sixth and the beginning of the fourth century B.C. that we can learn the particulars of marriage and family life. The father dominated, and all male children were trained to emulate him. Women's status was very low. The total repression of women created dull marriage partners. Often, heavy societal pressure was required to induce men to marry these uninteresting partners. The poet Palladas succinctly summarized the Greek male tradition when he noted that the married man's joyous days were limited to two: "the day he takes his bride to bed and the day he lays her in her grave."

A Greek story of the period told of an ideal wife through a character, Ischomachus. An elderly man, Ischomachus chose in a careful, rational fashion a fourteen-year-old girl as his bride. Both parties had reviewed the marraige marketplace and selected each other without any sense of romance. Besides children, Ischomachus sought "that their possessions shall be in the best condition possible, and that as much as possible shall be added . . . by fair and honorable means." There was no emotional interaction between the two. She ran the household so as to maximize the gain from anything Ischomachus brought to her.

The repression of women in ancient Greece was paralleled by another phenomenon—homosexuality. Often to avoid the unattractive option of marrying a sheltered girl, usually young and inexperienced, wealthy older Greek men chose males in the age range from twelve to twenty. For the Greeks, such a relationship had more than carnal intent. The older lover felt a passionate desire to teach and inspire his young lover to become a worthy man. It was as though a longing for procreation could be transformed into the desire of an educated masculine man to create a copy of himself in his student. Some men of ancient Greece preferred this life to having their own children with a wife.

Homosexuality was but one outcome of mate-selection methods. The age-different unions that often resulted caused unique consequences of their own in some cases. Unusual attitudes towards age-different couples were a part of the historical legacy.

During the Age of Reason, the 1600s and 1700s, the problem of the impotent husband was first observed as a social phenomenon. A suspected cause lay in the large number of aging men married to young, spirited wives. This ditty of the day reveals the frustration of the young brides:

> You wed us with a fancied fire
> To gratify a base desire,
> And take a Virgin to your bed
> With vigour—only in the head.[3]

This same period spurred the discovery and rediscovery of a host of tonics to restore the faltering ardor of an older husband. Diets began to include plenty of egg yolks, cock testicles, shrimp, oysters, chocolate, and milk.

Young women began to discuss openly with each other the provocations used to stir an indifferent husband. Some older men fought back, claiming that "too frequent sexual activity is also a problem since it dulls the sight, decays the memory, induces gout, palsies, enervates and renders effeminate the whole body, and shortens life."

Of course, we have our modern-day aphrodisiacs and ways of

helping unresponding males, but the French during those times took a practical approach. A husband accused by his wife of impotence was required to demonstrate his ability at intercourse before an appointed panel, or face divorce. Contemporary sex therapists, take note.

John Milton was born in 1608. I've chosen him as the grand example of an age-different relationship of the period. He was a scholar to the core, and his life-style went something like this: up at 4:00 A.M., reading from the Bible and studying until dinner, more studying, an hour of walking, organ playing, and then early to bed to repeat the regime the next day.

His poetry was sometimes sensuous, but always intellectual, and not unsurprisingly he arrived at his thirty-fourth year still a virgin. Milton's writings suggest that he overidealized sex, and that his lack of experience did not prepare his judgment for choosing a mate.

Milton expected a madonna. He selected Mary, seventeen years younger, high spirited, unintellectual, and with no political keenness. It is possible that the marriage was never consummated. In any case, after a month of Milton's schedule, Mary went to visit her parents and never returned. Stunned, then bitter and frustrated, but tied to his wife by the Angelican code which did not permit divorce, Milton poured his energy into writing *Doctrine and Discipline of Divorce*. Out of his pain and anguish came a classic tome, but his was not an age-different relationship to emulate.

Other models of husbands and wives, not necessarily new but certainly more visible, emerged during the Age of Reason.

Bernard Murstein describes the ideal husband of that period in this way:

> For the most part, a man's physical qualities were secondary; good financial status was necessary, but not sufficient. He should also be seven to ten years older than his spouse. All his time should be devoted to business affairs, but he must not become a dandy who spends his leisure hours at the hounds or talks of nothing but dances and duels. He was not expected to inspire passion but, rather, to be kindly and fatherly.[4]

At the same time women were beginning to climb out from under men's thumbs and assert new roles in marriage. It was easier if you were an older, wealthy woman like Mrs. Millamant in William Congreve's play *The Way of the World,* and were demanding certain freedoms from a young man as a prerequisite to marriage:

> I should like liberty to pay and receive visits to and from whom I please; to write and receive letters without interrogatories or wry faces on your part; to wear what I please; and choose conversation with regard only to my own taste; to have no obligation upon me to converse with wits that I don't like, because they are your acquaintances; or to be intimate with fools, because they may be your relations. Come to dinner when I please; dine in my dressing room when I'm out of humor, without giving a reason. To have my closet inviolate; to be sole empress of my tea-table, which you must never presume to approach without first asking leave. And lastly, wherever I am, you shall always knock at the door before you come in. These articles subscribed, if I continue to endure you a little longer, I may by degrees dwindle into a wife.[5]

There were a number of nineteenth-century experiments in marriage in the United States. From my viewpoint, the Oneida community in New York was one of the most interesting. The members believed that pleasure was the primary goal of intercourse, and bearing children only secondary. Unfortunately, they coupled this intriguing belief with the conviction that any useless emission of semen violated nature. It seemed like being offered riches, but not being allowed to spend them. Their convoluted solution: intercourse without male emission.

Stubbornly claiming that a trained man could stop at any stage of sexual intercourse, the community also dictated that the young should mate with the old as a way of achieving a spiritual uplift in an "ascending fellowship." Young men were trained with older, menopausal women. Population was controlled during early difficult times in the community, and critics claimed that free love was rampant at Oneida. However, those age-different couples flourished under complex sexual mores. Apparently it all worked, for there were no known cases of infidelity. After about thirty-three years, when the leaders had aged and the young were weak in their conviction, the community collapsed.

There is very little useful information, particularly specific data, about marital age differences in the United States during the nineteenth century. We have the hearsay evidence, such as:

A traveler here in the 1830's, Miss Martineau, was "struck with the great number of New England women whom I saw married to men old enough to be their fathers." [6]

We also have the marriage registration reports of the time. Unfortunately, the ages were given in five-year divisions, and there was no separation of first marriages from all other types. This problem was perpetuated into the twentieth century as late as the 1940s by the U.S. Census. Sociologists and demographers have worked with the data to extract more detail, and concluded that marriage age differences varied according to the region, ethnic background, occupation, and probably with time. Of course, large age differences can be detected even with the five-year increment. For example, 1930 U.S. Census data reveals that for husbands aged forty to forty-five, their under-thirty-five wives were one third of the nonwhite wives in Georgia, one quarter of the white wives in Georgia, and 15 percent of the white wives of Pennsylvania. Hardly startling statistics, but an indicator of age-different activity.

Boston stands out in its insight about marriage data. This city published a table showing the relative ages of married couples in the year 1845. Even though these data are in the five-year age groups, a rough comparison can be made with the 1934–36 data for the same city. These figures display a shrinking—though only modest—of the age difference for couples getting married.

Finally, in 1949 some data was taken which tried to account for the impact of remarriage on age difference. Among all married couples in the country, 18 to 74 years of age, 7.9 percent had an age difference of more than ten years (male older) for first-marriages. This jumped to 27.6 percent if the husband and/or wife had previously been married.

The wife older by five years statistic was 1.5 percent for first marriages and 6.7 percent for previously married. Other data prove that for all age-different couples, the age difference increases as the age of marrying increases. Apparently as people age, earlier cultural conditioning falls away.

In 1938 Dr. C. A. Anderson published a report which gave evidence that the age difference in premarital and extramarital love affairs was at least as much as in marriages. Later studies suggest it's even larger.

Some writers have attempted to use the skimpy data to connect the pattern of age-different variations to social changes and national crises. The period between the Civil War and World War I is considered the dawn of women's liberation and the modern American marriage. The major issues of the time were questions of free love as opposed to wedlock, the role of women in society, and the decision as to whether divorce should be made easy or difficult to obtain.

The "free love" adherents believed that each person should be free to live his/her own life without governmental regulation. Both anarchists and socialists supported this position for political expediency. The anarchists' stand seems obvious, but the socialists took a more complex posture. They said capitalism was the foe of marriage. How could people get married or be comfortable in a marriage if getting or keeping a job constantly concerned them? A new era of socialism offered an end to the humiliation of women and a more fair trial for monogamy. Most of the other reformists argued about whether marriage was a private affair, or that each individual "had a duty to marry, to preserve the fabric of society, and to rear sons and daughters for the sustenance of the republic."

Prior to the Civil War there was almost no divorce in the United States. By 1920 the number of divorces had increased by almost 2,300 percent in those sixty years. Four major forces allowed this to happen. Women had more options to be self-supporting because of expanded employment opportunities. Their legal status was improved by legislation. More available educational opportunities helped women strengthen their job credentials. And social ideology was slowly changing and encouraging the treatment of women as equals of men.

In 1924 Dr. W. Baber was the first to write about the data on age difference in relationships. In those days it was fashionable for sociologists to study such conjectures as "there is a trend today for career women to marry men eight to ten years younger." During the Depression, almost no useful studies were done. It was as though the age-difference research was as unsettled as the times.

A number of writers speculated that the Depression affected the age-difference pattern by delaying marriages. This delay caused men to marry much younger women than they might have earlier. Women of that painful period presumably reinforced the men's actions by having economic motives to marry much older and better-established men.

Astonishingly, this speculation about relationships during the 1930s grew out of the only work done during that period, a master's thesis by Dr. W. C. McKain. Later work by McKain and Anderson drew very different conclusions. They claimed that men were marrying women nearer their own ages because of "the sobering effect of adversity, the limitation of social fluidity and contacts in the Depression, the emphasis upon comradeship and mutuality of persons of the same age, and other such factors." [7] All of this is pure fantasy, and would be laughed at by researchers of today. There was very little useful data available. The investigators' line of reasoning is fascinating, however.

During the late 1930s and early 1940s, modest theories attempting to explain the increase in the number of age-different marriages were being advanced. It was accepted as a premise that the male in our society, upon whom the decision to marry generally rested, chose to marry younger women as he grew older. Admitted, the greatest supply of unmarried females was in the younger ages, but it seemed clear that the male preferred younger women. Theorists touted the fact that single women over twenty-five experienced a rapidly vanishing opportunity for marriage. For the educated or career women, their late availability left only younger men and the frowns of society.

Occupation appeared to make a difference in the formation of age-different marriages, but which way wasn't clear. "Marriages with significant age differences were more common in the upper classes," reported Anderson in 1938, but data published in 1948 indicated the reverse. One intriguing study by Terman observed large age differences at marriage for a large group of gifted youth.[8]

As theoretical interest in age-different relationships grew, older data were exhumed and manipulated to shed some light on the phenomenon. Some of the problems of these data have already been discussed. Not yet mentioned is the fact that men and women frequently falsify their ages on marriage records to avoid public comment and to be more in conformity with social attitudes. I believe that these falsehoods were more common in the distant past than recently, and that they do not significantly affect averages.

Summarizing hundreds of years of age-different mating practices is not as difficult as it seems. When women and men are free to choose mates independent of any cultural, economic, or religious constraints, for many the age factor is of no concern. As people age, and experience other relationships, older attitudes give way, and they more frequently choose age-different partners. Perhaps the biggest changes in age-different relationships through the years have been in the openness of the couples and their distribution over the entire social class range rather than being concentrated at the top and bottom.

J. R. Udry, in *The Social Context of Marriage,* writes:

> The utter inconsistency of the results forces one to conclude that the relative age of the mates is not a significant factor in the success of the marriage. People evidently have preferences in the relative age of spouses, and these preferences do not materially affect marital outcome. One might predict that the marriages would take on different interaction patterns in accordance with the age differences, and some research has found this to be true.[9]

CHAPTER FOUR

A Different Kind of Marriage

THE HOLY STATE of matrimony has taken many forms across cultures and through time. So many, in fact, that I would be at a loss trying to explain an earth marriage to a visitor from outer space.

The leading expert on the subject, Bernard Murstein, says:

> Marriage is a socially legitimate sexual union, begun with a public announcement and undertaken with some idea of permanence; it is assumed with a more or less explicit marriage contract, which spells out reciprocal rights and obligations between spouses, and between the spouses and their future children.[1]

Obviously, in this statement of marriage, with suitable definition of various words and phrases, just about anything is possible—and just about every kind of marriage has existed through history.

Today you can find group marriages, marriages in which couples swap partners, marriages that exist in communes where free sex is encouraged, childless ones and polygamous unions, unmarried marrieds and homosexual spouses, corporate marriages involving detailed written contracts, and, of course, the age-different marriages. The variations on the form of marriage appear endless, perhaps even suggesting that the title of this chapter is meaningless. However, despite the creativity of couples in finding social contracts that work for them, there is but one dominant form of wedlock in this country. It needs no description, and most of you know that more than a third of traditional marriages fail.

You also know that the traditional coeval marriage carries with it an enormous superstructure of other customs and constraints. But we are interested in the age-different couples, and their marriages are different in that once they challenge the age-similar custom and deal with the stigma that accompanies that action, other societal foibles and traditions often fall away.

Among the age-different marriges the most typical couple is the middle-class pair—she's thirtyish and he's fiftyish. Let's meet our first couple, Dot and Bill, and explore what's so different.

Some age-different couples can "pass" but Dot and Bill cannot. Anywhere you saw them, the difference in their ages would be apparent. Dot is an attractive, perky thirty. Bill is a poised, slow-moving, distinguished fifty-eight. As they walk down the street, she is literally in orbit around him, emotionally and physically.

Dot and Bill live so far out in the suburbs that they call their house a ranch. It's on ten acres where horses, and even cattle, have been kept. The setup is faintly monied, orchestrated with overtones of do-it-yourself and weekend-ranching. Their rustic two-story ranch house is nicely furnished, though messy throughout. Jes and I arrived just as the sun set.

With their children's sounds coming faintly from another part of the house, Dot quickly, and Bill slowly, began to share the details of their three-year marriage. Complementing their age difference was a startling difference in their backgrounds. Dot's childhood was a horror, and she escaped at seventeen only to recreate the same type of horror in her first marriage. Bill, on the other hand, was raised by sensitive, loving parents. His first marriage lasted thirty years.

Some details are pertinent. In Dot's family, her mother was the boss. Her father, who worked nights, appeared during the day only to inflict the punishments demanded by the matriarch. Only then, in those dreadful moments after the spanking, could her father say, "I love you." Dot's father hid his feelings for years, until one day he and the wife of his closest friend went to Mexico, divorced their respective spouses, and married each other. The abandoned husband and wife wailed their remorse to each other—then they married. Now, I'm told, everyone is friends again.

These events occurred after Dot, at seventeen, married her first husband, who was twenty years old. Two failures at running away from her parents, and the rejection of her request for a foster home, launched Dot into a marriage with a dominating husband. After nine years of "living under my husband's thumb and being his object," Dot and her spouse agreed to divorce. She convinced him to support her until she was able to earn her own living. Dot took real estate training, obtained a license, located a job in a realtor's office, and found Bill. She is convinced that her life was some kind of a vicious circle that ended only when she met Bill.

Bill, then fifty-four, was probably at the peak of his adult powers. Dot describes him as "contained and slightly standoffish . . . not on the ego trip of the supersalesman but soft-spoken and gentle." Bill, by middle-class American standards, had lived a good life. Raised in an upper-middle-class Irish family, he went through the Depression years with no real sense of strife. His father at forty had married his mother, then thirty years old. The father's well-established business meant a childhood of sailboats and racing outboards.

With great enthusiasm, Bill told me the story of how he, in those Depression days, traded his outboard motor for flying lessons and received his flying license at age seventeen. That was the beginning of a career associated with aviation—first, in the navy during World War II; then with the airlines; next, many years of operating his own aircraft instrumentation company; and finally, senior-management years with a large corporation. There had been a thirty-year marriage which was amicably allowed to die when the partners admitted to each other that there seemed to be no more reason to be together. Now, slowed down, and savoring life more, he was selling real estate part time and pottering around his ranch.

He and Dot, in the natural flow of their office contacts, developed a nurturing friendship. With each recently liberated from unfulfilling long-term relationships, they enjoyed the talks, lunches, and clean, lucid, adult interaction. "It was as though we had known each other all our lives," Dot said.

After some months, they became lovers. Their age difference was never a factor to be talked through—it just didn't seem to matter. Dot philosophized a bit to me and summarized the point better than I can.

"As you go through life you reach certain plateaus, then later when you grow a little and move to another plateau, you lose contact with people. It's not that you shove them off, but you are growing and they aren't changing with you. You can't just hang on! Bill was settled, knew what he wanted, was sure of himself, wanted to let me grow and go as far as I could—try anything I wanted to—and he promised me he would always back me up."

Nine months after they met, Dot brought her children to the ranch, where they lived for a year before she and Bill married. Simultaneously, Jes and I blurted out, "Why did you marry?"

Dot replied, "I married for the security of the children."

Bill and Dot seem to have an idyllic marriage. They use a middle-class formula, but loosen it enormously. They both take for granted a great deal of individual freedom. While they maintain many separate friends and activities, the bond between them seems to guarantee that each gets what she/he wants from the other.

Bill glides, but Dot bounces. We started to probe how those two styles fit together.

QUESTION: In general, how do you feel about the opposite sex?

DOT: I'm a man-oriented woman. At a party I talk to the men. Most women, after talking about their children, their last operation, and what bums their husbands are, have nothing else to say.

BILL: I'm a one-woman man, but I'm never jealous of Dot. If I can't hold her it's my fault, not hers.

QUESTION: It's likely that Dot will be a young widow. How do you feel about that?

DOT: My children will be grown and gone, and then it's my life. I'm going to prepare myself. I'm not going to be a lonely person in this big house. [*She is stuttering a little.*] I know I'll never find another man like Bill. [*He interjects:* "Oh, baloney. Lots of them out there. You just haven't met them."] I want to go on in school, get a degree and develop myself.

BILL: She'll find another great guy—she's so attractive and has good judgment. I don't worry about Dot being an early widow. She is plenty resourceful and will be okay.

DOT: My mother kept asking me what I would do if something happened to Bill—say in five years. I told her that five years of real happiness is worth it, because I lived through ten years of hell with my first husband. Even one good year would be enough.

QUESTION: What about the in-between time when perhaps Bill's energy and interests are flagging?

BILL [*protesting*]: I come from sturdy stock. We talked about it before we were married, and neither of us is concerned.

DOT [*As she began to speak we realized she was answering the question mainly from the viewpoint of sex.*]: When we started going together I admit that I wondered what the sex would be like. Whether his age would make any difference in bed.

BILL [*laughing*]: I never did undress in the closet, did I?

DOT: I wondered whether we would make love once a week on Saturday night or what. But our love life is fabulous—he is so aware and sensitive. He is able to satisfy my every whim and still take care of his own needs completely. I've never known a man who could do both. We have talked about what I would do if, at a later stage, Bill couldn't satisfy me any longer. I'm not a demanding woman. It's my responsibility to adjust. If I'm emotionally satisfied, the sexual satisfaction is no big deal. Sex is not the most important part of the relationship. Bill has encouraged me to have a lover if sex ever becomes a problem, but I don't think that's fair.

BILL: Modern man places too much emphasis on the value of sex. I believe a woman can get just as much satisfaction through emotions as from sex [*preachy—with tinges of hopefulness*].

DOT: When I'm at my sexual peak, Bill will be about seventy, and if he's slowed down, we are going to find alternatives [*very emphatic*].

QUESTION: You mean involving other people?

DOT: No. [*Confused and fuzzy here.*] I mean there are lots of other things we can do.

BILL: Read adult books? [*Chuckling.*]

QUESTION: You mean such as mutual masturbation, oral sex, and maybe using sexual paraphernalia.

DOT: Yeah, I guess. Or we could learn to give beautiful sensual massages. Just let the erotic times be different.

BILL: Whips and chains?

DOT: Be serious! [*And makes an obscene gesture to Bill.*]

BILL: People, no matter what their ages, will never have problems in bed as long as they remain flexible. Sure, I admit we're kind of dumb on the specifics, but we know that there is a whole world of possibilities outside conventional intercourse. And we have no hang-ups—we'll seek them out, learn them, and blend them into our own sex life as needed.

DOT: Absolutely.

QUESTION: How about having a child together?

BILL: The child would have to be an immaculate conception, 'cause we're both "fixed"!

DOT: When the step-grandchildren are around, people assume they're mine. I've got the best of both worlds.

QUESTION: Do you have any social problems because of your age-different marriage?

DOT: Very rarely, and then only from the older wives of some of Bill's business associates. They are people we don't know very well. The women give me the cold shoulder, but I ignore them. I smile and talk to their husbands, who always respond to me.

BILL: There is a scene that has been replayed in my office at least a dozen times. I'll be talking to a new client when he will notice Dot's picture on my desk and usually make a comment about my attractive daughter. When I tell him the photograph is of my wife, it's fascinating to watch the sequence of emotions. First, he's surprised, then mildly embarrassed at his mistake. He takes a closer look at the picture and admiration appears—followed by pure envy as he looks back at me. It happens most every time, and I love it!

QUESTION: What about friends?

BILL: I've never needed many friends, male or female. They've just never seemed important in my life.

DOT: I like people, and I have lots of friends, men and women. I visit them, meet them for lunch, and sometimes one of them drops by for a chat and a drink. If it's a man, it's no big deal for Bill.

BILL [being very pompous]: Most men don't have any real sense until they are over forty.

DOT: One day Bill asked me, "What are you going to do one day when I'm eighty, I'm drooling out of the side of my mouth, my zipper's unzipped, and I have egg on my vest?" I told him I was going to keep him hung up on a special gold hook in the closet, and make appointments to take him down and use him any time I needed. [Shiny-eyed and emotional now.]

BILL: The only concern I have is that as I grow older I may not be able to keep Dot happy, but I take that as a challenge that will help keep me young. I love her so much, and I want to keep her happy, and so I'm going to be very aware of her needs.

DOT: I've got the ultimate deal. I'm married to my best friend, and it's getting better all the time!

Dot and Bill are living examples of a theme we found common among age-different couples. They are absolutely clear about what they want from life and from each other, and they honor those needs. This view translates into invulnerable priorities and gives a solid frame upon which their marriage is built.

In the early 1970s, Nena O'Neill and George O'Neill, in their book *Open Marriage,* described an evolved version of the middle-class marriage:

Open marriage means an honest and open relationship between two people, based on the equal freedom and identity of both partners. It involves a verbal, intellectual and emotional commitment to the right of each to grow as an individual within the marriage.[2]

The union of Dot and Bill embodies these characteristics. Each is his/her own person. Their identities are not blurred. At their stages in life, they have reached across the generation gap and fused bonds emanating from their complementary needs. Without even trying, Bill has discovered a universal truth. Because he and Dot have matched complementary stages that firmly ground the marriage, allowing Dot her freedom only strengthens their ties. The world is filled with weak marriages that survive, at least temporarily, because of the constraints placed on either or both mates.

In 1977, in *The Marriage Premise,* Nena O'Neill wrote:

> In describing our model for an ideal marriage of equality, George and I devoted the book to suggesting how couples might build a relationship of trust, intimacy, and commitment through true sharing and caring. As an entirely optional consideration, and not as an integral part of our model for an open marriage, we opened up the topic of outside relationships.[3]

Outside relationships are a natural part of age-different unions. Each partner is likely to have a coeval set of friends, and the energy from these contacts only strengthens their intense loyalty to the marriage.

Erica Jong, that outspoken writer on topical issues, touches the nerve ending of another difference in age-different marriages in these sentences.

> There are three major reasons why the nature of marriage has changed today, and all of them derive from technology and the changes it has wrought in our society. First, women rarely die in childbirth; second, all people live longer; and third, childbearing and rearing occupy a decade or two rather than a whole lifetime.[4]

Nineteenth- and twentieth-century popular psychology, until very recently, had unwaveringly postulated that a woman cannot find fulfillment unless she has a baby. Technology has indirectly supported that position by making childbearing easier and safer. We have, however, in this country, a large group of late-to-marry, career-oriented men and women who are much less certain about the sacrosanct assumption that when we grow up we will be parents. And we have a core of people involved in age-different romances and marriages who genuinely make child rearing an option.

This is an important point, because it is patently clear that the biological limitation for a woman to have a child safely past her late thirties represents a very practical flaw in age-different relationships, if having a child is a high priority.

Throughout my own youth, I heard women, and sometimes men, speak in hushed tones about the powerful drive within women "to procreate and preserve the species." I was taught that such an urge might be latent for years, but ultimately it would surface and have to be allowed to function. Today it is well understood that not every woman is suited for a career as a mother. The psychological effects of parenthood for some women raise serious questions about their continued good mental health. And, of course, it's difficult to drum up much support for the preservation of the species in these times of perceived overpopulation.

Most age-different couples face the issue of having a child, not as a given, but right along with concerns about separate careers and finances, outside relationships, monogamy, identity, social pressures, early widow(er)hood, and the impact of the aging of one partner.

If there is a single phrase which characterizes the age-different couples we know, it is "lack of exploitation." An interlocking network of complementary needs seems to work against such exploitation. These couples sense that the preservation of a sense of equality is absolutely critical to the health of their relationships. Nowhere is this more true than in money matters. This is the arena in which so many clichés about old-young alliances have been spawned. "He [she] just married her [him] for her [his] money." This particular truism came from the time when servant girls flashed shy smiles at the lord of the manor.

Once again, Erica Jong has wise words on this matter.

All expenses would be shared, fifty-fifty if possible, and if not, prorated on the basis of the earnings of each. The remainder would be banked or invested, each partner having his or her own hoard and possibly having one joint hoard for joint purchases and projects. All child care would be shared if possible, and if not, prorated on the basis of differing amounts of free time, including remunerated and unremunerated labor. All child-care expenses would similarly be shared. At the time of the union the partners would agree in writing on how to dispose fairly of joint property at the time of dissolution of the marriage, if ever.[5]

Very few age-different couples, I suspect, have read Jong's opinions. However, acting intuitively, they have created in their plan of marriage many of these principles. Critics might say that the scheme sounds like a preparation for failure, and in that way encourages termination. Not so. Just knowing that such an agreement exists encourages longevity for the relationship because of the implicit permanent sense of equality and lack of exploitation.

These financial arrangements have two specific thrusts within the general theme. In the first one, the person who stays home and raises the family is protected, and in the second case, in a two-career family, the member with the lesser economic leverage is safeguarded. Because the second case is the more common one among age-different couples, we will focus on these issues.

As reasonable and humanistic as the financial strategy appears, it contains fatal flaws which appear upon use.

Jane, thirty, a flight attendant, and Joe, fifty-two, an airline pilot, have been married for three years, after a six-month trial period of living together. As we will see, they appear to be very different people. However, they have developed slowly, and sometimes painfully, a remarkably successful marriage. I want to focus on how they handle money matters.

Joe, married twice previously, bears grotesque psychic scars from those marital experiences. Jane likens their getting together as equivalent to the effort required "to melt the polar ice cap." Joe, settled and happy as a single, never expected to marry again. The dominant element in his fear and aversion was money. For more than fifteen years he had staggered under the load of child-support and alimony payments, and when Jane came into his life and began talking wedded bliss, he froze. It all took time, of course, but Joe came to recognize how much this beautiful young woman had to offer, and how his life was enriched from just being with her.

Jane's background was totally different. Her position with the airline was her first "real job," and she had just begun when they met. Never married, for most of the previous decade she had been a sometime-student supported, in part, by a string of part-time and short-term jobs. Lovers helped out along the way, and the backup of doting parents was always there. She was a compulsive spender, and planning was not her strong point.

Jane had deflected marriage proposals many times, and "chose Joe very carefully." She knew of Joe's sensitivities and assumed they would work things out.

First, no children. Joe had three to fit into their busy schedules when time allowed.

Then Joe concocted a document which said that anything acquired with his effort and income would always be his, and she would never make any claims. The reverse was true for her. Jane signed. After all, she was a liberated woman who suported the idea of justice for each sex.

Next Joe proposed a financial plan in which each, on a prorated basis, contributed money for the operation of the household. After all, Joe earned four times as much as Jane.

Joe insisted that they keep separate bank accounts, and that any large item purchased be owned by one or the other—no joint ownership. Jane knew that Joe was willing to buy and furnish a house.

Finally, he suggested that if either one had money troubles, the other would help out with no-interest loans. Jane knew this was for her benefit, because she could not imagine Joe needing any of her money.

How did all this work out? Let's hear it just as I taped it in an interview with Joe.

I admit it. I have a very complex attitude towards money, and I suspect it's getting more complicated all the time. I love Jane so much, but I felt I had to be true to myself and protect my tender parts. I knew that if I weren't up-front with my limitations I would ultimately damage our relationship.

I have never understood the idea that the moment a marriage ceremony is over, each partner shares equally in all the assets of the other. I don't believe it should be taken for granted, but worked out and agreed upon, just as every other facet of a relationship. Jane knows how I feel, accepts it, but her romantic notion of love believes that underneath all my intellectualizing, I will share everything with her if push comes to shove. When I made out my will, some of that attitude emerged.

In a way, she has forced me into the role her mother played. No matter how much her mother ranted and raved about Jane's spending habit, Jane assumed that her mother would share everything with her. All my life, the buck stopped with me. I've never had any financial backup, and I'm convinced that my life was all the better for it. Jane is on her own, financially, except possibly for a serious emergency.

We've tried the idea of sharing equally, according to our capability in all our expenses. There is a serious complicating factor in this arrangement, and it's so obvious. Getting the money together is one thing, but how it is spent hinges on the values of the individuals involved, and most people have different spending habits.

For instance, we know about how much our food will cost, so we both contribute, my four dollars to her one, and form a food kitty. However, we split all chores, and depending on who does the shopping, the pantry and the refrigerator look very different. I plan each meal and buy for only a few days at a time. Jane does large shopping with many snacks and treats, lays in an inventory, and improvises at each meal. When Jane shops, it's feast at the first part of the month, and famine at the end.

I suppose all this sounds a bit silly, but we are committed to equal justice for the partners in our marriage, and it's not so easy. I like a simple house, Jane is more ostentatious. I dress casually, Jane more dressy. I like low-key vacations, Jane more exotic. And I'm losing interest in material possessions, Jane is not.

Most of these qualities complement one another and generate a lot of interest and excitement in our life together, but financially it's a mess. Each of us wants individuality, but after we do the simple arithmetic of money division, all hell breaks loose!

The aftermath of what I've just described leads to our last problem in money matters. After we equitably set up the money for regular household expenses, it takes care and planning to make it through the month with our personal expenses. I'm good at it, but Jane isn't. With a week to go in the month, I'm doing fine, and she's broke.

We both know she can borrow from me, but that seems a crass thing to do for such small amounts of money. So, slowly but surely, I start picking up more bills, and the financial obligation subtly shifts until our equality is damaged. And this happens again and again.

The strangest thing occurs at the same time. Almost without our awareness, I do less housework and Jane does more. Finally, at the end of some months, we've transformed into a traditional marriage. Then we laugh at our not-so-subtle compensations, renew our money vows, and try again.

Listening to Joe's talk of sharing expenses makes the "benevolent dictatorships" that exist in many middle-class marriages more understandable. Joe and Jane know that they are on the track of something valuable for their marriage. Each must learn new skills, and soften old attitudes.

A fascinating connection that we noticed during the research for this book was the similarity between age-different married couples and couples who cohabit. I call them the "unmarried marrieds." Cohabiting couples who live as husband and wife are testing many of the innovations described earlier in this chapter. The number of cohabiting households has more than doubled since 1970; however, the esimated 1.1 million couples are only a small fraction of the 48 million or so traditional husband-wife households. There are no estimates of age-different partners among the cohabitors. We found that many couples who were age-different and were living in a long-term marriage-like arrangement did not agree philosophically with the legalistic aspects of marriage.

Social scientists believe that cohabitation is a form of protest against the conventional constraints of marriage. Cohabitation has become a favorite dissertation subject for PhD students. There is even a newsletter published on the subject. For unmarried people to share a residence is against the law in twenty states. But that law is like the one that makes it a crime for unmarried people to have intercourse—rarely enforced.

In our interviews with cohabiting age-different couples we found an intriguing variation on a theme as old as social contracts between people. "Social contracts" may sound stuffy, but that's an appropriate term for the arrangements made between partners in a couple. Sometimes the contract is prearranged and visible; other times it's assumed. Sometimes the details come from special requirements of the individuals; other times the contract is based on social custom.

The critical ingredient in this coupling contract is money. But not like the money issues of Jane and Joe, our previous couple. We all know about mistresses (misters are less common): people who live in or out and provide sex and possibly other services for money. And most of us are aware that loveless, sagging middle-class marriages, in which wives receive special budgets or "allowances," are accused of being nothing more than a form of prostitution. The topics are sex and money, and it would be difficult to find two more sensitive taboo areas in our culture. Sexual issues are more out in the open the last decade, but money is still "in the closet."

The theme underlying the next type of age-different couple is that you can buy affection. These couples have come together largely on a financial basis, and they live healthy, productive lives together by using money as the medium.

In 1974 Edmund Van Dusen wrote a book, *Contract Cohabitation,* in which he described yet another variation on the affection-for-money theme. His book was not limited to age-different couples, but many of his points are pertinent. He said in an interview:

> I'm not talking about the sexual companionship relationship —leave sex out of it! My book has almost nothing about sex in it. It deals entirely with companionship, emotional support, the things that a human being has to have to function effectively, because we're a social species. And so, he's prohibited by our mores from using his strong point (money) and forced to go back to an earlier era of his own life to compete for companionship and emotional support on an eighteen-year-old level, and this is totally destroying. . . .[6]

Van Dusen was referring to the "plight" of the financially stable older man who, after divorce, finds himself back coping in the world of singles. His solution was to advertise and seek exactly the services he wanted—for pay.

The age-different couples we found were not quite of that ilk. They were more like the classic older, never-married, divorced, or widowed man who has a live-in housekeeper with a very broad range of duties.

Paul is one of my favorite people. In his seventies now, and essentially inactive in his small publishing business, he lives the good life. A simple home in a canyon near a small mountain range is the focal point where Paul and his friends meet. Paul's life revolves around his friends—either in correspondence or with a steady stream of visitors. The man is a blatant womanizer. Two marriages have not dulled his enthusiasm. He is constantly on the prowl, and a young woman will capture his attention regardless of the circumstances. Men in his life are often angered by his erratic attention, but I got over it long ago. Through Paul, I have met fascinating people.

As you might suspect, most of Paul's romances are brief. He chooses women who are too young, too pretty, and definitely on the move. And they flit quickly through his life. In recent years, he unwittingly pushed away women who felt genuine affection for him, but would not tolerate his incessant sexual energy, or his desire to "trap" them for himself. Finally Paul got the message. He had aged to a stage where he needed assistance with housekeeping chores. This, in addition to the fact that he was alienating too many women, caused the changes. Now he maintains a delicate balance with live-in salaried housekeepers, who sometimes act as lovers but are mostly friends. They are usually very young "liberated women."

This age-different relationship is difficult to describe. Paul's "companions" filter out of his network of friends and usually stay a year or two. On a casual, cooperative basis, Paul and each companion do what needs to be done. They nurture each other physically and emotionally, take care of his house, and entertain his friends. Even though a salary is involved, the basis of the contract is friendship, and therefore Paul is very flexible and undemanding.

In spite of the fact that the term is fairly short, this kind of relationship is a marvelous example of matching opposite stages.

Both people usually need assistance—Paul has paid for college tuitions, airplane tickets, and car installments. In exchange, he has received typing, gardening, cooking, and housekeeping services. Perhaps I'm describing an "age-different barter," but whatever this relationship is called, its foundation of mutual caring and concern makes it impressive to observe.

A variation on Paul's age-different relationship is the older man who marries his "girl Friday." Another out-of-vogue label, a girl (could be boy) Friday serves as a special assistant to a busy person, usually performing a wide variety of chores and generally serving as a confidant. The type we encountered most frequently was an older man, characteristically an artist or writer, but usually self-employed and successful, who was married to the young woman who performed all his "support services." She was lover, companion, secretary, hostess, housekeeper, and whatever. These unions developed when a former employee or lover changed roles.

The final "different age-different marriage" to be described is based on a teacher-student scenario that isn't at all apparent upon meeting Peter and Trish. They are very attractive people with an astonishing presence. It's clear they have an age difference, but not at all obvious that it is twenty-five years. They have been married for five years and have a three-year-old daughter.

Peter was forty-three and a well-known therapist when he met Trish, who was eighteen. Peter's life was enviable. He lived in the country on a lovely inherited estate about two hours' drive from New York. He and a small professional staff gave workshops for couples needing counseling, and worked with individuals on a wide range of life problems during short live-in stays. He was in demand as a therapist, and there were always more requests for his time than there were accommodations available. I knew Peter long before he met Trish, and always envied his ability to attract the beautiful women who were in his life. Eventually, I learned that a brief, annulled, teenage marriage seemed to have soured him on that institution.

Trish came for a weekend workshop held by another therapist, but met and liked Peter. Interestingly, she was seeking counseling at the end of a two-year love affair with a man of forty-two. A few months later, at Peter's urging, she returned and spent a week in therapy with him. Peter described her as "sorrowing, confused, and absolutely unclear about what to do with her life." When the therapy session was over, Trish stayed on for a few days and they became lovers. A few weeks later, Trish returned to live with Peter.

It's difficult to imagine two more different people. Peter was well educated, sophisticated, confident, and successful. Trish, a high school graduate with no special skills, simply wanted to get married and have children. She called her maternal urge "overpowering." These opposites developed genuine affection for each other, even as they played their game of tug-of-war. Trish incessantly lobbied for marriage and children, while Peter, suspecting strong insightful powers in Trish, tried to involve her in a training program for therapists. In short, she wanted him to be a father and he wanted her to be his protégé.

Eventually Trish did become Peter's student, and assisted him in group therapy sessions and in couple counseling. They were a perfect counterpoint to each other, Peter with his cool, distant reserve and rapier-like analysis, and Trish with her warm, open, loving approach to people. In effect, each became the other's therapist. Trish helped Peter explore his deep fear of commitment and marriage, and he helped her clear out a towering set of needs and expectations no mate could ever hope to meet.

They had been together for about a year when Trish became pregnant. Her contraceptive protection had failed, and the accident elated Trish and depressed Peter. He was, however, still the teacher, and she the student. His arguments prevailed and in two months Trish had an abortion. Those were very hard times for them. Their powerful emotional connection seemed weakened by other forces. They retreated to their work, and went on with their teacher-student life.

Months later, Trish's moaning woke Peter in the middle of the night. She twisted and tossed as Peter watched, trying to imagine her dream. Eventually her hips began to move, swinging her pelvis up and down. Then Trish said, in a voice not like her own, "I want to come out." Peter told me how the movements and the words went on and on, building to a crescendo, until in one final convulsive thrust Trish threw herself upwards, shuddered, fell back limp, and woke in Peter's arms. They both knew they had experienced the symbolic birth of their lost child conceived nine months earlier. Peter looked at Trish and simply said, "Will you marry me?"

In that very dramatic way both Peter and Trish transcended the parts of their pasts that blocked them from each other. Peter's fears were softened by being witness to the deep involvement and sincerity of Trish's love. And Trish, living through a period of intense maternal desire, found other ways of strengthening her tie to Peter.

With Trish nodding agreement, Peter said, "The work we do together as teacher and student is our primary bond—a special kind of loving. I feel it is much more important than any conventional ties implied by marriage. At some point in the future, if Trish decided to be with a younger man, our special loving would not be affected."

And Trish added, "Peter is my friend, my lover, and my husband, but first and foremost he's my teacher."

As we talked and explored their feelings about marriage, Trish spoke about the value to her of formalizing their union through marriage. "It was important to me to make explicit to the world what was implicit. I felt certain that eventually we would have a child, and I wanted our child to be able to point to us and say, 'That's my mommy, and that's my daddy, and we are a family.' I wanted us to be able to join hands, form a circle, and know that the circle was strong and permanent."

Two years later they did have a daughter, Tina, and we asked Peter what it was like to have his first child when he was in his late forties.

"Well, it was a bit of a crisis for me. Not because of my age, but just becoming a father shook me up. Previously, I had always thought of the people in my therapy groups as my children. They weren't, of course, but my own child would be a new element and possibly some interference in the progress of my groups. I imagined the child wanting more from me than I could give, and I feared Trish would be distracted from our professional work. These things didn't happen. The first year was very tough. We were exhausted constantly, but there was so much learning in it for me. I've never been around children much. In fact, I've never thought I was allowed to be a child, and it gave me great pleasure to give that to Tina, and to learn to play and be childlike with her sometimes."

QUESTION: Does it worry you that when Tina is twenty, you'll be nearly seventy?

PETER: No, but I knew that if I were going to have a child, I probably shouldn't delay any longer.

QUESTION: Peter, do you ever feel jealous of your beautiful young wife?

TRISH: He is very unjealous. I'm the jealous one. I'm the one who has all the dreams about him going off with other ladies.

QUESTION: Younger women?

TRISH: Oh, no. Age has nothing to do with it. They are always dark-haired, short and very competent, especially in their emotional beings. I'm so emotional! With me, everything is a high, a low, or a crisis. I constantly overreact. The women I dream Peter with are always really solid and don't need him very much— wouldn't make any difference if he walked away. And if he spent time with another woman, they would never be upset. They are everything I'm not! [*Laughing.*]

After we had talked to Trish and Peter for nearly three hours and were about to leave, Trish wanted to continue. I switched on the recorder, and she began a long, rambling monologue. Here are some excerpts:

I want to tell you about something I watch in myself. The sooner I let go of it, the happier I will be. Sometimes, in an ordinary conversation, a woman from Peter's past will be mentioned. Without any warning I will tremble from spasms going through my body. I'm getting better about dealing with it, but I usually sit down and cry hard for a few minutes. Peter waits quietly and hands me the handkerchief. I use my tears to wash out of me something I don't handle well. If I had met Peter when I was forty, and we were both forty-eight now, I would have had a lot of relationships prior to this, and I would have a history like his. I frighten myself thinking of all those people Peter was intimate with before I came on the scene. All those women he was excited about and made love to. And I'm afraid I'm going to be left out in some way. When I pay attention to how much we love each other, and how fortunate we are, that kind of scene just doesn't come up. It would be absurd for me to tell a counter-story about a boy I had a crush on in junior high school! I know that these fears will die when my insides get the message that there is nothing to fear about being alone. It doesn't really have anything to do with Peter. My fear of being alone probably came from something that happened when I was two years old, and I have to clean it up. When I truly understand that I've got me— then I'll be okay.

At this point we interjected a question: "Do you ever feel the need to develop more of a 'history' of your own?"

TRISH: No, I occasionally get attracted to somebody. It upsets me terribly when it happens. So I just go home, tell Peter what's happening, and we talk it out. We both recognize that there are wonderfully attractive people in this world who will catch our eye, but we have an agreement of fidelity. I feel so blessed by our relationship. I have with Peter everything that I ever dreamed about in a man when I was a romantic fourteen-year-old. I've got every bit of that, and I never stop being amazed. I have a fairy tale dream come true. I feel so lucky to be in a really trusting, genuine relationship with someone I'm growing more trusting with and learning to love more every day. If there is anything abnormal about our marriage, let's find out what it is and teach other people how to be abnormal.

I'll never forget the psychiatrist my parents sent me to see when I was a teenager and seeing an older man. He told me if I were loving a man that much older than me, it must be incestuous. It meant I was really loving my father, and that loving anyone older than twenty-three was incestuous. I was so confused, I burst into tears. He came around his desk, gave me some tissue—and then made a pass at me. I couldn't believe it!

The critical characteristic that we detected in the age-different couples of this chapter is the self-esteem of the partners. They seem clear about who they are and what they want to do. In various ways they all told us that a commitment to another person, in any kind of relationship, does not have to be threatening if each partner has a strong sense of self-worth.

CHAPTER FIVE

November-December Lovers

ALL OF US will be old someday. Yet it is astonishing how little we, as individuals and as a culture, know about being old. Anne Simon, in *The New Years,* writes:

> The subject of getting older has a power of its own, a power which can make an otherwise rational person irrational. It distorts fact, releases savagery, imperiously dominates good sense with nonsense. Throughout history it has fascinated and repelled, causing men to devise marvelous schemes by which to avoid their own aging and mystical systems by which to accept it. It has accumulated a great, impenetrable aura of myth, superstition, and fiction around itself, so grand and imposing that the events of this century which might, at long last, unseat the power, have instead fueled it.[1]

Simon's words, written a bit more than a decade ago, are essentially true today. A few things have happened. Just as poverty was exposed finally in this country in the 1960s, the aged were discovered in the 1970s. Both were there all along, of course, but neither poor people nor old folks fit well into the model of the American dream. Or so people thought, anyway, because in that curious way our nation deals with undesirable matters, both groups were rendered invisible for a long time.

Gerontology is important today. Reports on studying the aged are on every new book list, magazines and journals flourish, and dollars from research foundations promise understanding where there was none.

It's not clear what will come of all this effort. So many damning trends need to be overcome. The worship-of-youth cult, the widespread acceptance of the idea of nonwork for the last third of life, the ghettos of the aged forming a subculture apart from the mainstream of national life, and a general unawareness of what it means to be old are a few examples.

Although earlier I discredited the research on adult developmental stages as being too shallow to provide much assistance, it is worthwhile to cite some studies as they apply to the aged. In *Human Development,* written by Justin Pikunas, a tabular form lists the "developmental task" for every age. For late adulthood (women forty-five to sixty years old, men aged fifty to sixty-five), he writes:

Adjustments to family changes as children leave home; preservation of adult personality traits and abilities; preparation for retirement.

Regarding women from age sixty to death, and men from sixty-five to death, he states:

Maintaining frequent contact with children and grandchildren; maintenance of health; integration through maintenance of self-esteem.[2]

The above is hardly a clear picture of the last third of anyone's life. Let's delve deeper into the aged condition in order to understand its impact on forming age-different relationships. Two stereotypes struggle for supremacy in describing older people. First, as we age we become what we have always been—only more so. We have an unchanging image: overachiever, extrovert, cold fish—it doesn't matter. When we have more time and money, we just do more of it.

The second stereotype insists that the influence of late-blooming insight and the consummate wisdom of the elderly cause us to reverse our image. We must emulate youth, release materialism, and give up bowling.

A person's life experience at any age in any stage is a consequence of who one has been, modified by how one interacts with social and cultural factors. The elderly are not excluded. Just as with any age group, we expect to find a wide range of biological, personal, and social maturities present.

Anne Simon says: "To the common experience of getting older which all who live share, each man brings his own uncommon imprint."[3] So we are back where we started in one sense. Just as with all other stages, we have a large group of people, all in the same chronological age range, yet each quite capable of living out unique life experiences.

To get a feeling for the aged, we must explore the levels of maturity they present and the physical and cultural impact of the environment on their mating practices.

First, let's take personality, which represents the fit between a person and his unique social world. The theories conflict. Researchers describe personality as "both relatively stable and continuous, as well as relatively flexible and changeable." As a person ages, the outside social world fades in importance, and the more internal world of the individual is revealed. In 1933, Carl Jung wrote in his classic book *The Stages of Life:*

> Ageing people should know that their lives are not mounting and expanding, but that an inexorable inner process enforces the contraction of life. For a young person it is almost a sin, or at least a danger to be too preoccupied with himself; but for the ageing person it is a duty and necessity to devote serious attention to himself. After having lavished its light upon the world, the sun withdraws its rays in order to illuminate itself.[4]

Data on post-fifty personality adjustments also suggest that a kind of turning inward occurs. People tend to avoid change, to be intolerant of ambiguity, and to be less susceptible to social pressure. But let's be cautious and not create another stereotype.

As activities fall away for the older person, life is simpler. Personality traits are much more visible, and people become "bigger than life." Identity for the elderly does not derive from being a banker, having ten children, or swimming Lake Erie. Life is more basic, and we can more easily know who the elderly are, what they need, and what their expectations are.

The elderly are often characterized as moving toward more eccentric, self-preoccupied positions as they attend increasingly to the control and satisfaction of personal needs. My description takes a slightly different form. Older people are less concerned about society's attempts to control their lives, and they are more acutely aware of their own needs than in any earlier period. The result is many prime candidates among the elderly for age-different relationships, in which the selection constraints are fewer.

One of the characteristics frequently observed in people as they age is an increasing interest in locating a confidant. The confidant provides services most individuals probably need, but old folks are very clear about his importance. He is someone to talk to, a buffer against the changes implicit in aging, a companion, a helper, a lover, and maybe all these qualities wrapped up in one person— a spouse.

Erik Erikson takes another slant on the subject. He says, "Adult man is so constituted as to need to be needed lest he suffer the mental deformation of self-absorption, in which he becomes his own infant and pet." He goes on, "The fashionable insistence on dramatizing the dependence of children on adults often blinds us to the dependence of the older generation on the younger one." [5]

As we age, the enormity of satisfying specific personal needs becomes clear through the haze of economic and social constraints. In the absence of a confidant, Bernard Berenson wrote of a different solution in his diary:

An individual without something to cherish scarcely exists. For most people, what counts is children. Lacking offspring, they take to animals and live entirely for their dogs, their canary birds, a pet monkey, or most unexpected of all, a hare.

Authors of several research studies have been unable to resist a desire to categorize the ways in which the elderly deal with aging. The successful agers were called "mature," "rocking-chair," or "armored." The "mature," by far the largest group, slipped into old age with little neurotic conflict, high self-esteem, and genuine satisfaction in activities and personal relationships. The "rocking-chair" men and women approached life passively, and were happy to be free of responsibility. The "armored" adjusted well to aging by remaining very active as a defense against passivity or helplessness.

Advanced years were not pleasant for the "angry" and the "self-haters." The anger of the "angry" came from failing to achieve their life goals, and their disappointments were aimed at others. The "self-haters" also missed their goals, but directed their resentments against themselves.

What can we do with these categories? We might try to use them as a kind of fine structure to give some specificity to the advanced adult stage. The trouble with this is that it's too easy to think of people who are blends of two or more types. Like the "armored hater," someone who will work indignantly to his or her death trying to reach unattainable goals.

Perhaps the most useful result is the recognition that the four groups, not including "mature," had aging problems from lifelong personality sets. And curiously, the "mature" did a mild reversal. They were ordinary—stable personalities with some personal adjustment difficulties; they mellowed with age. Facts are, however, men and women from any group may and do seek an age-different partner. Knowing which category each person is in will probably improve the quality of the matching.

Biologically, we know little about what causes aging. We must, therefore, concentrate on the effects of aging and see how these influence later-life mating. We do know, for example, that the rural Scandinavian woman, who does farm work for twelve hours almost every day, will live twenty-five to thirty-five years longer than a single, American urban male office manager who is a heavy smoker.

Hardin Jones constructed a table in which the impact of a

variety of factors on longevity is listed. Country versus city living will give you five years. Being married is another five. Having four grandparents live to eighty is worth four years. But being epileptic knocks off twenty years.

I doubt that anyone forms his living pattern from selecting a set of controllable factors that are said to increase life span. A greater concern is the quality of life rather than the length—or so say many of the people we interviewed. Yet in the next moment they admit that they want to be around as long as possible to enjoy that high quality.

The signs of getting older were observed and cataloged in early medical records—and the record keepers have never stopped. The greatest complexity in interpreting these signs lies in the fact that aging and disease are interwoven and defy disentanglement. That means that the physical, personal, and social development we want to observe is influenced not only by the individual's past life experiences, culture, and physical environment, but also by the incidence and effect of disease.

The presence of all these potentially influential factors has delayed any clear understanding of the process of aging. There may be some value for us in reviewing a list of acute and chronic conditions that appear more frequently as an individual ages, but it would be very difficult to interpret that information. Or, we could study data that show that with advancing age the body becomes less efficient in sensing, processing, and responding to external sensations. But we already know that.

It will be more useful to continue to review the basic qualities likely to have the greatest effect on latter-day mating—personality, intelligence, and sexual powers. Of course, some will be concerned about health and wealth, but idealistically speaking, these will mean little without the first three.

What about intellect? Read Anne Simon's words:

> The crucial power of these years is intelligence and the crucial fact is that the capacity for intelligence remains unchanged. The line of the mind does not follow the vital animal curve which traces the body's fast growth and long, gradual decline. Instead, it rises slowly, lifted by learning, to a plateau which stretches across the adult years. Each man has a capacity of mind that

is his when he draws his first breath and his last, unless it is destroyed by disease or finally blotted out by senility somewhere in between.[6]

Certainly, old folks may get a bit slower at intellectual tasks, but the power is all there. Short-term memory may falter, and learning will take more time, but motivation, interest, or the lack of a recent educational experience is more likely involved in the delay.

Let's get on to sexuality. It is on this topic that the stereotype of aging is most tenacious. Novelists and poets have done us all a disservice by praising the elderly couple, with all carnal passion dead, walking quietly hand in hand down the road to the end of the journey into the sunset.

This image, implanted in the minds of many by their childhood readings, often persists until the urgings of their own lives reveal its dishonesty. To conceive of sexual relations between elderly people is deeply shocking for too many people.

The alternative, however, has been the "dirty old man." It is curious that the theatric tradition which endlessly used the theme of the aging male lover in a satirical way was closer to the truth than the playwrights ever imagined.

Another alternative was to be accused (again the man), "He's in his second childhood." This allegation admitted that the man remained sexed—but impotent, like an infant.

It is absurd to think of old people as condemned to chastity. There are too many memories from the past, not to mention the temptations of the present, to relegate sexual activity to mothballs. For most people, their sexuality was a chief source of pleasure and a critical part of their images. The attachment to an earlier erotic world, and the longing for more experience, is still there.

The early sexual lives of all people are not always so positive, and age may offer an excuse to withdraw. As the body ages, disappointment may cause men and women to be unavailable physically. And, of course, there is the force of public opinion. The risk of ridicule possible for being a sexy senior citizen will sometimes turn off the most stalwart lover.

Then there are the statistics. Sexual intercourse diminishes in frequency with age. The averages are presented in solemn reports in which the loss of genital power and the interactions of psychological factors are analyzed. What does this mean? Very little. Sex for the aging man involves a set of factors that can create a wide range of sexiness that lies beyond the frequency of intercourse.

Of course, there is the erection issue. Most men, most of their lives, have felt the pressure, as well as the pleasure, of sexual performance. Rare is the man who has not at some time failed to erect when either he or his lady fervently desired him to do so. The aftermath of such a failure can range from derision to rejection. Add to this the folk myth which insists that an aged penis is more often a limp penis, and an older man may carry the inherited baggage of ambivalence towards sex.

If he is married, rather than unmarried or widowed, his rate of intercourse is greater. Married life generally lowers the emotional barriers. The male is usually free to choose the time of lovemaking, and a failure is no big deal. Anxiety, that heat that melts the sturdiest erection, is less common among married men.

Many an older man returns to the comfort and simplicity of masturbation. His wife's aging body no longer attracts him, or she may, for various reasons, turn against physical love. The wives of working men seem to enjoy longer, richer love lives than the spouses of more wealthy, sedentary overachievers.

The most significant influence on the sexual life of aging men and women is the richness and happiness of their earlier sexual life. For that reason, the sexual mores of older people are primarily a combination of aging and society's attitudes towards sex at any age. Both of these may act to diminish the strong biological power that is still there. Many men seek indirect forms of satisfaction—erotic literature, the company of young women, various forms of perversion, and voyeurism.

Biologically, women's sexuality is less affected than men's. Studies by Kinsey and by Masters and Johnson describe the sexual stability of women through the years, and cite the fact that foreplay and intercourse are highly valued, even if orgasm does not follow. The aging of a man's body seems of little concern. Even though the aging woman's sexual interest wanes little, her frequency of intercourse falls off. Men who do not flag often take to younger women. Such opportunities for elderly women are less frequent.

Researching the subject of aging sexuality was fascinating. The literature reflected our culture's tenseness about sex and old folks.

Even when the material was saying that there was no biological limitation and that the psychological problems came from society, the presentations themselves seemed curiously cold.

A wonderfully refreshing exception is *The Tao of Love and Sex: The Ancient Chinese Way to Ecstasy,* by Jolan Chang. Crossing the cultural boundary seems to help.

> . . . a relationship between an older man and a young woman has some real advantages. First, an older man is often slow to erect in response to foreplay. For him, a young woman who produces ample vaginal lubrication quickly is a blessing. He can insert his phallus into her vagina without a full erection more easily. After entering such a lush environment, it is a simple matter for a man who knows the Tao to become fully erect. And on her part she may find such a gentle, slower procedure enchanting and preferable to a young man's frighteningly sudden erection, abrupt insertion and swift ejaculation. . . . Just as he is slow to erect, he is slower to finish, an essential factor, which could bring her to an ecstatic bliss and which many inexperienced young men are not able to do. . . .
>
> Sometimes older women find it hard to keep going through vigorous and sustained lovemaking. Sometimes their vaginas cannot supply sufficient lubrication, usually one or two short lovemaking periods in an evening is all they can manage.[7]

Chang writes of "the gentleness and experience" of the older woman. As he writes of the age-different relationship of older men and women, he deals with their sexuality in a clear, direct way.

Another element to consider before meeting some November-December lovers is economic. Women who are receiving their deceased husbands' full Social Security benefits are cut to half if they remarry. The alternative, in their jargon, is "shacking up," and they hate it.

The law forces them to violate that strong sense of personal and public morality ingrained in older Americans. "Social Security has driven us to sin," they say. More and more older couples who want to be together are convincing compassionate clergymen to perform a ceremony of marriage—without including the marriage license. They find that going through the ritual is reassuring.

In these last pages I've summarized the characteristics of aged people. Who they are is one matter, but where they are is quite another. They are in a culture which caused Morton Puner, in *To the Good Long Life,* to make this statement:

> There are two great invalid and destructive myths about the old. One is the idea held by almost all young and middle-aged persons, that a new marriage for the elderly is foolish and inappropriate. The second myth is that sexual joy is reserved for for those in the first decades of life. These myths are so pervasive and powerful that they have caused millions of older persons to live lives of loneliness and frustration.[8]

Duke University's Erdman Palmore collected jokes based on these myths. Here are some samples from the thousands circulating in our culture:

> *On declining mental ability:* Four stages of memory loss: forget names; forget faces; forget to zip up fly; forget to zip down fly.
>
> *Definition of old age:* the time of life when a man flirts with girls, but can't remember why.
>
> *Description of the sexual life cycle of a man:* triweekly, try weekly, try weakly.
>
> *Definition of an old maid:* a lemon that has never been squeezed.
>
> *An old woman was held up by a robber,* who proceeded to frisk her for money. After a thorough search all over her body, he gave up. She exclaimed, "Heavens, young man, don't stop now—I'll write you a check!" [9]

Tasteless humor is one of the milder cultural and social forces that shape, restrain, and threaten the elderly. Although many older women are interested in marriage or remarriage, there is an extreme shortage of older men. In the fifty-five to sixty-four group, there are abouty eighty men to every hundred women; by sixty-five to seventy-four, about seventy-two men to every hundred women; after seventy-five, only sixty-three men to every hundred women.

There are four times as many widows as widowers, and three

quarters of those widows are sixty or older. If a man survives his wife, he is instantly a prize in an unbalanced marriage market. After sixty, age differences have little meaning, and age-different couples are common. Among the elderly, age difference in couples is no more a basis of discussion than weight difference. For that reason, exploring the lives and mating practices of elderly age-different partners is about the same as for the average aging couple. In a market where more than two thirds of men over sixty-five are married but only one third of the women are, something has to give, and the age barrier crumbles.

Another element that complicates matching among oldsters is the double standard of aging. The social convention that aging enhances a man but progressively deteriorates a woman tempts many women to lie about their ages. Some women never leave their fifties, thus creating age-different marriages if they wait long enough.

Both older men and women share another obstacle to remarriage. Memories, good and bad, of a departed mate may stand in the way. The survivor of a marriage that was marked by a long period of invalidism or chronic illness at the end may fear a repeat of that scenario. Guilt over betraying the memory of a happy marriage is another block.

And children are no help. There is an almost universal attitude among younger people that a new marriage for one of their elderly parents is stupid and inappropriate. They fear another marriage may fail, or sever their own relationships to their parents; they worry about a threat to their inheritances. Sociologist Dr. James Peterson wrote, "Some [children] feel that their mother or father ought to spend the remaining years in celibacy in honor of the deceased mate."

Unfortunately, these and other negative pressures hurt lonely and isolated elderly people when they are most vulnerable. But the desire for love, and the satisfaction of personal needs, are powerful motivators. More and more elderly couples live together or marry in secret.

One couple we interviewed admitted that their marriage, when she was in her middle fifties and he in his middle seventies, prevented his children from putting him in a rest home. Another couple married only after signing agreements leaving their estates to their respective children. With their children reassured, they were free to get from each other what they wanted most—love and companionship.

We talked to one man of ninety-five who was ninety when he married his wife, seventy-four. In my naivete I tried to question him about using remarriage as a kind of proof of enduring masculinity. They both gently resisted talking about sexual matters, but as we chatted, I realized that their sex life extended beyond the bedroom. He spoke of her perfume, a pat on his behind when he took out the garbage, and just being there when he felt blue. She relaxed then, and became shiny-eyed as she talked about "having him tramp around the house. I don't even mind his muddy boots and the ashes from his pipe."

Some November-December couples admitted getting married because of money. The crunch of inflation encourage a finances-companionship barter. Most couples had short courtships, small and quiet or secret weddings, and often no honeymoon. This low profile beginning usually didn't last. Once the age-different mates were comfortable with their new status, they wanted everyone to know. They gaves parties during which an eavesdropper might hear phrases such as "love at first sight" and "head over heels in love."

We asked all the November-December couples we interviewed what it took to make such a marriage work. Most were liberal with their advice, and there was an astonishing similarity of views. Success hinged on four qualities: the bride and groom knowing each other very well before marriage; having the approval of friends and relatives; each having enough money; and each partner being well adjusted and generally satisfied with life.

Trouble often struck November-December couples who kept separate financial accounts or lived in a house belonging to either mate in a previous marriage. Almost no statistics exist to pinpoint the failures of November-December marriages. The few studies we found suggested a 6 percent age-different failure rate, or less than one fifth the national divorce rate.

The most common November-December mates we found were seventyish men married to fiftyish women. Typically, both had been married previously, but had lost their spouses through death or divorce.

Hal and Helen are such a couple. When Jesalee and I met them Helen, fifty-seven, a former divorcee, had been married for seven years to Hal, seventy-seven, a widower. Helen told about a short wartime marriage which failed miserably: "After the war we went to live with his parents, who ordered me about like a servant, while he treated me as chattel. No Irish girl would stand for that—so that was the end of a terrible mistake. I left." Helen worked for twenty-five years in secretarial and office positions. She led a life she described as "responsible and solid—not as exciting as I might have wanted. Most of all, I regret that I had no children."

She considers herself one of the first liberated women: "I was pushing doors open, paying my own check, and telephoning men for dates when that wasn't so common. And age had nothing to do with the people who were in my life and close to me. If I liked someone, I never thought of age."

Helen presented herself in a rather open, forceful way. She stood slim and straight, and spoke loudly with carefully enunciated words. Her presence was in marked contrast to Hal's; he was small and quiet, and spent most of the time slumped in a chair. We soon learned that Hal needs help getting up from the chair because of his bad knees.

Hal has an incredible long-term memory. As we talked, he told story after story filled with precise detail. Every few minutes, when he came to a poignant memory, his eyes filled with tears and his voice choked. No one said anything, and he soon continued.

Hal is the survivor of a family of thirteen children. Hal's mother was forty-eight, and his father forty-nine, at his birth. Hal, a minister's son, married young and stayed married to the same woman for forty-eight years. She died a few years before he met Helen.

Hal's life is undistinguished. He had little education, raised a daughter who went to college, and worked all his life in minor administrative jobs in government and business. The highlight of his life seems to have been his foreign assignments for the government.

Hal reminds me of my grandfather. He radiates the values of an earlier time—work hard, children should be seen and not heard, honor your parents, and be good at all costs. He talks about his views as though they are immovable, and suggests that they deny him access to many things happening today.

Hal drifted after his wife died. Retired and fairly comfortable except for chronic arthritis, he painted his house so many times he got tired of it. He's a good cook and housekeeper, but works slowly. Helen and Hal were introduced by friends. Their relationship grew slowly, though Helen claims she knew from the beginning that they would marry. For over six months, she called him Mister, and he called her Miss. The next six months were a little more familiar, but not much.

After a year, the two married in the face of stiff resistance from Hal's daughter. She felt Hal was unfaithful to the memory of her mother. Helen continued working, and Hal became a house-husband. Helen says that family and friends took little notice of their age difference. The only comments were shallow, as "What about when you want to dance, and he's in a wheelchair?"

Hal's daughter, Betty, and Helen are near the same age. In previous years there have been uncomfortable moments when the two women were thought by an outsider to be sisters. Helen laughed, and Betty fumed. Hal seems oblivious.

In a few years Helen will retire. Let's fantasize about their life when Helen is sixty and Hal is eighty. Their small, attractive home in the suburbs is paid for, and they will have no serious financial worries. Helen has a wide circle of active friends with whom she will do extensive traveling. Hal will happily tend his gardens, take care of the home, and be there for Helen when she returns. Helen loves Hal's grandchildren, and will do as much mothering of them as may be allowed.

They will get exactly what they want—and with a little bit of luck my fantasy will come true. In the long term, Hal's health will ultimately limit them. Perhaps a few years of the fantasy will be followed by a nurse-invalid life. Helen and Hal have made their peace with the fact that their remaining life together will be short and, possibly, difficult.

Our next age-different couple, Joe and Beth, run a used buggy lot. On a sunny afternoon we walked through the collection of buggies, kicking dust with every step, and occasionally spooking a chicken from beside a spoked wheel. Joe talked about the buggies and wagons as though they were old friends. He related their history—where they'd been and what had happened. There were stories of stage lines, mines, rodeos, and parades.

Some models were dilapidated and rusty. "Haven't got to 'em yet," Joe said. On others, the gilt shone and the fringe fluttered, inviting passengers. Curious horses in the adjacent corral poked their heads through the rail to get our attention.

Behind the buggies was a stable, and through an open door I saw rows of polished leather harnesses hanging on the wall. It would be easy to imagine that we had gone back in time at least a hundred years, until we completed our tour and were looking back toward the road. Sitting squat and somehow tawdry next to the lively buggies was a modern mobile home—the "bunkhouse" for Joe and Beth.

Joe, like his father before him, worked with horses all his life. He never knew, or wanted, anything else. Five minutes after I met the man, he was telling me the story of his father driving, at age twelve, a twelve-horse rig on a freight line through the nearby mountains. That was a long time ago, because Joe is seventy-five, and his father was fifty-nine when he was born.

Until just before World War II, Joe's father supplied all the horses needed by a nearby city. Joe told me that his father dug the cellar for the city hall with horse-drawn machinery, but that was the end. After that everything went to engine-driven equipment.

Joe has done everything one can do with horses. He raised, trained, and sold them. For years he raced horses and was on the rodeo circuit. He makes and mends harnesses, restores old wagons, carriages, and buggies, and rides in parades. He shoes horses and leads horseback excursions. He says horses are "twelve-hundred-pound babies," and he loves them.

Anachronistic, you might say. Joe seems to have forgotten what century it is. That isn't true. He knows. Embodied in Joe are centuries of the skills involved in working with horses, and he has found ways of using them today. He is tough, independent, self-sufficient, and down-to-earth. Until a few years ago, Joe was a sour man. Now he is married, to a microbiologist twenty years younger than he.

His former causticity came from two short, painful marriages—one in his thirties and another in his forties. Two children from the first marriage and another from the second complicated his life in a way that he won't even discuss.

In his fifties, when the anguish in his life had eased a bit, he found himself. He had an excellent reputation in his business, his trailer home to take with him, and all the skills and inclination to take care of himself. His life was filled with rodeos, shows, parades, expositions, and trips, but always there were the horses and his snug trailer to return to at night.

Joe's uniqueness brought a steady stream of people to him, but "none of the women ever pleased me," he said. He stayed alone and liked it, until he met Beth.

Beth loves horses, too. However, she had a successful career working for pharmaceutical companies. Well educated and dedicated to her profession, in spite of "a few close misses" she never married. Her life was that of an overachieving company person. Sixty-hour weeks, traveling on business, and the endless effort of staying up-to-date in a fast-moving profession dominated her life. Teaching horseback riding was a weekend luxury.

Beth was raised on army posts. Her father, a high-ranking officer, was rarely around. The family unit, however, was tight and emotionally strong. Her mother did the difficult day-to-day job of raising three children. Their rare times with their father were treasured. Beth commented, "He never struck us—he looked at us, frowned, and got instant obedience. Even though we live miles apart now, the family is still very close."

Beth and Joe's beginning was not very romantic—they met at a mule show. Beth and her sister had brought a mule to compete in the show, and tagging along was her sister's Australian shepherd dog. Beth describes meeting Joe in this way:

My sister and I and her dog were standing watching one of the showings. Joe walked up and asked about the dog. "What's it to you?" my sister quipped, in her usual style. It turned out Joe once had a dog just like hers, and he was looking for a pup. Her dog was spayed, but miracle of miracles, I had a pregnant shepherd at home. Right then, I agreed that he could have one of the pups.

Weeks later, Joe received his dog from Beth and promised to call and keep her informed of the pup's progress. Beth admitted that, although their meetings were purely business, "the wheels were turning."

Kelly, the pup, did well, but when Joe called Beth, the news was sad. Kelly had been stolen, and months later, through a strange twist of circumstances, Joe recovered her. The animal had been run over by a car. After major efforts to save her, she finally had to be put away.

Things developed slowly between Joe and Beth. By telephone, they shared the anguish of Kelly's tragic life, but they lived in different worlds. At that time Joe was working the racetrack circuit —a few months in each town. Beth, in her white coat, shiny laboratory, and big city, saw the world through different eyes.

Over a year later, Joe called to say he had bought a small ranch and was looking for another dog. As Beth tells it, she had no idea where to get a dog, but assured him she did. Beth searched until she found a pup, bought it, and gave it to Joe. That was the romantic beginning for both Joe and Beth. During this period changes had taken place in their lives. Joe was tired of traveling, and Beth was very disenchanted with the work-and-money-oriented world in which she lived. In a gradual way, each began to anticipate contact with the other. Neither ever mentioned age.

Two years after Joe and Beth met at the mule show, they married. Although they spent weekends together for several months, their courtship was no whirlwind. They seem to have met just at the time when each was leaving one stage of life for another. They maintained contact through the transition, and the match worked.

Joe left his nomadic, lonely life, and Beth turned away from her career in order to join him in a new life on the ranch. Beth's avocation of teaching riding became a full-time job, and Joe possessed all the other horse-oriented skills. They are the "Ma and Pa" of the horse business, and their mutual respect is evident. Beth and Joe have complementary horse activities, often with different hours. They share equally in all the other chores around the ranch. Joe said, "In order to make an operation like this work, you got to pull together." Beth added, "Joe never asked me to marry him— he asked me to be his partner."

Joe's health is not good, and chronic digestive problems make it difficult to eat away from home. He often dozes in the evening. Beth says, "Life is different in the country. Our friends understand Joe's limitations, and there is no need to go out and make social rounds as I did in the city. There is a constant flow of people through here during the day, and just spending time together being lazy in the evening is wonderful. We have everything here. It's not like in the city, where you're always looking for some way to be entertained."

Joe and Beth talked at length about the joy of being together. Joe's assessment was startling. "For the first time in my life, I have some understanding of why a person might take his own life. When I think of our few years together, compared to the quality of most of the rest of my life, I wouldn't want to live without Beth. [*Both are teary.*] Our time together is so special, it doesn't make any difference what happens [*referring to his health*] or how long it lasts. We want to be together here."

"Every minute is precious," Beth summarized. And then she went on to say, "And I want to talk about sex."

QUESTION: What is your sex life like?

BETH: A great deal of mutual respect. We keep sex in proper perspective with the rest of our life. [*Both are talking at once.*]

JOE: We don't just jump in bed any old time.

BETH: Everything is super. We adjusted to each other very well. Joe had a bad experience with an urban princess some years ago, and he never quite got over that.

JOE: I don't mind having sex, but I don't like to talk about it.

BETH: The main thing we have learned is that in the big picture, neither sex or age is an important factor. It's your own thinking, your common interests, mutual respect, and willingness to adjust attitudes that makes any marriage work.

QUESTION: Do you fight much?

JOE: Hot and heavy for about two minutes.

BETH: Minor disagreements.

JOE: We don't hold a grudge. We let it go.

BETH [*emphatically*]: We never take arguments to bed.

Like any other subculture, older people gather in clusters. Sometimes it's in retirement communities. For those who need more assistance, a rest home is the place. The more people we talked to in these settings, the more we realized how frequently these people were forming partnerships, and how infrequently the age factor ever came up.

Sixty-four-year-old Martha is an example. Two years ago she married Elmer, eighty-nine. Elmer was napping when we arrived at the complex where they share an apartment, so Martha took us to the bright, attractive sunroom to chat. Her marriage ceremony had been performed a few feet from where we were sitting. Girlishness emerged as she described the details of the wedding. Here, in her own words, is the story of how Martha and Elmer got together.

When I came to live here four years ago, I was a mess. I had been widowed years ago, and was doing pretty good, but my health broke down. Finally, I got so bad that my family sent me here, where I could get proper care. You should have seen me. No teeth, just flapping gums, terribly overweight, and I didn't care how I looked.

I couldn't believe it when Elmer took an interest in me. I figured he just liked to rehabilitate old folks. We became close friends, and he advised and encouraged me on everything. He's kind of a health nut, so I started watching my diet. We went to exercise class together, and then he took me along on those long walks of his.

I loved the attention, and he seemed to enjoy my company. He convinced me I didn't have to look like a frump just because I was older, and I bought some new clothes. Then he sent me to a dermatologist for my bad skin, and to a grooming class.

When it was all over, I couldn't believe it. I don't believe I looked or felt any better when I was young. Our getting married was the most natural thing. We were together all the time, and got tired of running back and forth between our two places. Whenever I try to tell Elmer what he has done for me, he insists on thanking me for insuring that he will live to way past one hundred years!

Malcom is sixty-two, and we learned you can't be around him for more than five minutes before he tells you: "I have worked for fifty years, and expect to continue working till the end." Neatly attired in a gray tweed business suit, with a colorful bow tie, he talked to us in his fashionable retirement home near a golf course. The area is dominated by older people.

A businessman all his life, he worked for other companies until he started him own importing firm. As he chomped on a cigar and talked like a machine gun, I couldn't believe the cultured setting in which he lived. The house was filled with books and art, and even had a music room with a grand piano.

"You're probably wondering what I'm doing here," he said, grinning. "Everyone does." He went on to say, "It's the wife."

Candor is Malcolm's strong suit, and he openly shared the details of his three-and-one-half-year marriage to Mary. "Mary is eighty-two," he said a bit belligerently. "We've known each other for years. When I decided to move out here five years ago, she helped me fix up the place."

Mary came from academia. She was an art professor, and her deceased husband had been the president of a small liberal arts college.

Although they came from opposite ends of the intellectual world, Mary, Malcolm, and their spouses enjoyed casual social contacts for years. It sounded like a trade of vitality and culture.

A few years ago, when they were both widowed, Malcolm asked Mary to help him plan his new house and to make it reflect that side of life he had missed and which she knew so well. She did just that, and in doing so, made it their house.

Malcolm told of entertaining artists and authors, separate bedrooms, Sunday afternoon poetry readings, running his business from the den, and reading enthralling books he hadn't known existed.

His happiness was obvious, and the matching of the opposites successful.

CHAPTER SIX

The Odd Couples

IN MY FILE of material for this chapter is a letter torn from an advice column in a newspaper:

Dear Beth:

I am 21 and in love with a 13-year-old girl. She thinks she's in love with me. We were thrown together by a slew of rumors that we were carrying on, when we really were not. But as time went on we fell in love. I am close to her family and wouldn't do anything to hurt her. What shall I do about this sticky situation?

Mr. Stuck in the Middle

The columnist's advice was to the point:

> Stay away! Nothing good can come from such a relationship. You will hurt her by depriving her of her childhood. And you'll have to be the one to pull back because a young girl feels so much prestige is gained from attracting an older man. Show your maturity and stop this romance before it goes anywhere. Your needs are too different from hers. Your very presence urges her to try to act adult before she's ready. Do what you know is right.
>
> Beth [1]

No surprise there. Perhaps some of you would have given similar advice.

Many of the people Jesalee and I interviewed for this book responded to ads we placed in magazines and newspapers. They, in turn, referred us to others, and the ripples went on and on. From this age-difference network several unusual couples contacted us. These relationships are far off the mainstream of social life, but they demonstrate, even more graphically then typical pairs, how quickly age becomes a non-factor in the face of satisfying more extraordinary needs.

One group of men, usually in their early thirties, pursue girls in their early teens. That's making a twenty-year age difference the hard way, because the social resistance to such relationships is enormous. And the legal problems are even more dangerous. Complete secrecy is frequently a necessity in these alliances. As we talked to some of these men (the girls were never accessible), we were struck by some intriguing, if complicated, examples of matching complementary stages.

Gene did not come to us from our age-difference network. We had known and observed him with amazement for over two years, but not until the genesis of this book was it appropriate to ask him for any details about his life. Gene is a freelance carpenter, and our paths crossed often enough to develop a casual friendship. We also met his long-term teenage lover briefly, though we had no idea she was so young. Here is Gene's story in his words.

I am an adopted only child, so I never knew my real parents. My adopted parents loved me, and I'd label my childhood "normal." I did well in school, especially English, and the rest of my life was taken up with reading, playing my guitar and singing, and sports.

With my parents' support and my part-time work, I went on to college and majored in English literature. I fell in love with a classmate, a sweet midwestern girl, and we married during my junior year, when I was twenty and she was nineteen. We separated after graduation. Haven't seen or heard from her since, and I can hardly remember what she looks like. During the three years we lived together, she never once got off. My ego was hanging in shreds. I figured she had been traumatized by a puritanical mother at about age eight, and nothing I could do was any help.

I took a job teaching school to avoid the draft. For a year I lived in a little mining town in the mountains and taught Mexican-American children English and singing. It was very difficult, and I think I aged ten years during the one year.

Then I was accepted for graduate studies in Chicago. I hated the weather and the city. The so-called "prestigious department" was a disaster. Nothing but neurotics and alcoholics and young assistant professors running around saluting everyone. I spent hundreds of hours reading and that was wonderful, but I had to sort out the turkeys from the faculty and focus on the ones who had something to say. Studying the literature from the best minds of our culture was the only thing that preserved my sanity.

I never even talked to a woman that year at Chicago. I was burned out on women. My intellectual interests started to fade, too, and I found myself putting more energy into singing and playing in clubs around campus.

After I received my master's degree, I went to San Francisco. I ran into an old friend from my freshman days. We started dating, and before I knew it, I was married again at twenty-four.

It all seems a blur now. Here I was, twenty-six years old, working on a doctorate, married, paying homage to the work ethic every day, and all of a sudden I knew it was dead wrong for me. I hadn't learned enough in my first marriage to avoid repeating the same mistake again.

So I started some of the old patterns again. I hung out in the bars that had an open mike, and I'd play and sing for anyone who'd listen. I began to sound pretty good, and every now and then I'd be hired for a gig. I let the music suck me in. I was staying out late a lot, not paying much attention to my studies, and eventually both my wife and very straight in-laws began to complain.

One night after playing in a bar, a beautiful girl sat down at my table. We spent some time chatting and drinking wine, and then, as if it were prearranged, we left the bar, went to her place, and I spent the night.

The next morning I sensed that my life had been turned around. Somehow that little "skate on the wild side" made me realize how much I'd been holding my emotions down. I went home and tried to tell my wife what was happening to me. She couldn't understand what I was saying, but I insisted that I wanted to make changes.

It was all downhill for us after that. She stayed in the graduate-student, good-daughter, middle-class world, and my mind and emotions drifted. A couple of months before my twenty-eighth birthday I moved out, and that was the end of that.

Somehow I'd had a vision, starting that night with the strange girl, that my life could go other ways—ways that would be more right for me. In the aftermath of all that hard living, I passed through my twenty-eighth birthday, four times seven, and with a full moon to help me celebrate. I was in a small resort town in the mountains—my first visit to that beautiful place—and a local bistro was having its monthly astrological party. I was there with all the other Aries people, and on my birthday, under the full moon, I cut loose from that first twenty-eight-year Saturn cycle, and I knew my karma would change. It did. That was the night I met Ann. She was twelve years old.

I know it sounds corny, but that evening, and without my wanting it to, my entire life passed in review for me.

A weak, weepy mother, an always-traveling father, no dating
in high school, college life dominated by two women,
both of whom eventually became wives and ex-wives—and for
the first time in my life I was aware of the deep-seated
insecurity I had in relating to women.

I can't believe that I didn't know what a little boy I was
when it came to women. That emotional experience on my
birthday gave me the insight and strength to start searching
in an assertive way to see what I could do with my life. I felt
like I was back in junior high school and starting over. I
was hitting my emotional puberty.

Ann, at twelve, was just coming into her own sexual energy,
and I sensed it when we met. She was experiencing the
explosion that I had been sitting on and subverting for so
many years. At some deep level, at least for a moment, I
thought of her fresh, youthful sexuality as the water that had
been missing from the desert of my marriages and other
relationships.

In effect, I fell down on my knees and said, "I've got to
to have her." But of course I wasn't ready. Months passed,
and I developed a good business as a carpenter in the town.
A long-time hobby really helped me out.

One evening about six months later, I saw Ann a second
time. I was playing guitar in a local coffee house. She came in,
sat down, and began to listen. Before I knew it I was
playing just to her, and the rest of the people faded away.
I was brought back by my date insisting that we leave.
And later she told me she didn't want to see me anymore,
because "I know what's going to happen with that girl." ·

I thought she was nuts, but a couple of months later
when I saw Ann again, I instantly took her home and we went
to bed, and I knew I would hang on to her as long as I could.

I'm convinced that what happened with Ann could
never have happened if I were some twenty-eight-year-old
stud wanting to get it on with a young girl. We related as
equals. I was so hungry for her adolescent energy, and she
was so far ahead of her junior high school set that we
just clutched at each other.

For over three years we developed a close relationship.

Her mother was divorced and worked, and she was so busy
with her own social life that Ann had a lot of freedom.
Eventually her mother knew about me, of course, and after
initial uneasiness she became used to me. Ann and I were
always very careful where we went and what we did, and I
took a lot of pressure off Ann's mother.

In the beginning Ann and I were ageless for one another,
but after three years we both seemed to move into different
phases. She awoke my heart and then moved on. While we
were together we had a kind of high school romance. All
the jealousy, horsing around, and experimentation was there,
but eventually Ann needed to expand, meet other people,
and do other things. We started having as many lows as
highs, and we couldn't seem to break that pattern.

I still experience feelings of anguish when I see Ann with
someone else. With her I know that good, bad, or indifferent,
I'll have some contact with her the rest of my life. She is
the first woman I've ever met that I knew I could never
walk away from and completely forget.

Near the end of my relationship with Ann I slept with
with a few of her high school friends. They seemed to be
breaking out into the world, and there I was—right at their
level. During that period [*thirty-two*] I didn't date anyone
over sixteen. My friends seemed to accept what I was doing.
In fact, I suspect they envied me. I was bathing in the
brightness of the adolescent energy of those junior and senior
high school kids and loving it. Somehow I was able to be
that kind of brightness too. Some of my friends told me
that they had never had enough of that time in their own lives
before they had to shut it off. They considered me neurotic
to do what I was doing, and yet they were jealous of me.

Age had nothing to do with our eventual breakup. We
were simply heading in different directions at that point. Then
I started seeing women nearer my age. There were more
understanding and common experiences, but such jadedness
and lack of intensity for life. With older women, a million
other intellectual issues were present which mitigated and
diluted the head-on, man-woman connection we were both
after. I had experienced a kind of pure passion with no

hidden agendas of house, kids, job, blah, blah, blah. With a young girl it's all "being in love with love," because that's all you can possibly have.

Being with Ann opened up twenty years of blocked emotions. Once that erotic energy started flowing, it got aroused by all kinds of pretty girls. I found out that if I really allowed myself to accept the power of emotion and sensibility that another human being has to offer, I could never back off that position.

Now I'm with Lynn, who's fourteen. I met her when she was about nine. In those days she was a bright, gangly beanpole. Then she went to live with her father, and when she came back she had stepped into a twenty-year-old body. She's confident, poised, and very clear about her womanliness. She had lost her virginity long ago, and was ready for a serious relationship. She has had more sexual experiences than most young women come to marriage with.

Both Ann and Lynn came to me with a level of emotional and sexual experience beyond what I had. The excitement with them was not the deflowering of a virgin, but being part of the first time they experienced deep passionate love with no limits. Being the recipient of that kind of rich, deep love being delivered for the first time defies imagination. All the two of us wanted was love. It took my breath away!

Lynn's mother is threatening to send me to jail, but if that happens, I'll still say that I was part of something that I'm so glad I got to see. And my boss is putting pressure on me about going with underage girls, but I've finally learned, at this advanced stage of my life, that human beings are human beings and when you find somebody you respond to, you go for it. It doesn't matter if she is forty-five or fifteen. I can't guarantee I won't get involved with a seven-year-old next week.

Most people miss the main point. I fall in love with young girls. They don't see that we all are just boys and girls on the planet, and we are all complete and ready for love. Others don't understand that I respond to something profound in these girls. All they think I see is hard tits. After I 'awakened' with Ann, I'm now available to the world in a way I wasn't before.

Some people ask me if my fancy education gets in the way of relating to my girl friends. I've found that the hindrances and blocks that interfere with my young lovers are neither more numerous nor more significant than those I encounter with a male friend because he grew up in Brooklyn and I didn't. Differences of sensibility are there between any pair of people.

As I look around me, I observe that not many people match up, no matter what age. I've found ways of connecting to people so that our differences don't limit us. I perceive my lover's needs, and make mine known, and our relationship balances these against each other.

I'm in a stage of my life now, where young girls are in a unique position to give me that special romantic experience I need.

Claude is urbane, cultured, and witty. In his late seventies now, his successes in writing and painting have created a sophisticated group of friends for him. He has been married twice previously— at fifty-four to a woman thirty-one years younger, and at forty-seven to a woman fourteen years younger.

Claude's social skills are immense, and yet he has a complex passion for love affairs with young women aged twenty to twenty-five. In an unbelievably charming way, he can speak to a total (young and beautiful) stranger and include her in the activities of the moment or in his life—with scarcely a ripple of effort or difficulty.

At the beginning of his interview, Claude made it very clear that he had no intention of doing a monologue. He insisted that we ask him specific questions.

QUESTION: Why are you so attracted to young women?

CLAUDE: I was born and raised in Europe at the beginning of the century, and came to this country as a young man. My youth was spent in an unbelievably conservative and repressed environment. It was as though I had no youth as we think of it now. All my energies were devoted to just surviving. Up until 1929, it was incredibly difficult to meet women in this country. If you were lucky enough to meet someone legitimately, there was enormous pressure to marry. After the stock market crashed in 1929 and the economic crunch with its hard times came, social matters loosened up. Women became much easier to meet. It was as if some pretensions had fallen away. Economic stress is a great leveler. But back to your question—I suppose it is as though I've never stopped trying to make up for the emptiness of that early phase of my life.

QUESTION: That's an interesting and analytical answer, but it doesn't explain why you choose women in such a narrow age range.

CLAUDE: Let's be absolutely honest about this. Any single man chooses the most attractive woman he can get. It's perfectly natural. Under twenty, a woman is undeveloped in all ways; over twenty-five, women lose their freshness and become jaded after a series of lovers or a husband.

QUESTION: Don't you suspect that your craving for young beauty is an ego-boosting attempt?

CLAUDE: Of course, that's part of it. I never feel more powerful or more sure of myself than when I'm with a beautiful young woman. But don't forget that I give as much as I get. I can't tell you how many women have told me how they are turned off by incompetent young lovers who care only about themselves. An older man tries to satisfy the woman first—himself second.

QUESTION: Don't you suspect your ladies are seeking a father figure?

CLAUDE: Oh sure, that's part of it too. You know—the Electra complex. But don't forget that I can afford to do a lot more for a young woman than most young men can. I have the personal, social, and financial resources to offer them a great deal, and they know it.

QUESTION: Do you have any trouble talking or socializing with a young woman? I would think you'd have so little in common with them.

CLAUDE: Heavens, no—I take the role of a teacher. A teacher-student relationship is flexible, strong, timeless, and age makes absolutely no difference. Think about it. A teacher and a student can be friends, lovers, co-workers, companions, or confidants. The teacher-student bond is a special channel established for a unique needs exchange, and it exists quite independently of most everything else.

QUESTION: Do you ever fear that your lover will be stolen by a young man?

CLAUDE: You're asking about personal insecurity, and that can happen at any age. I think you're also asking about monogamy, and often that's not a realistic goal to pursue. I've never restricted my ladies from having other known lovers. I abhor secrecy. My experience is that other occasional sexual alliances merely strengthen our relationship. For me the main issue is the quality and amount of personal energy being exchanged between me and my lover. I'm not a demanding person, and as long as our union is healthy I don't much care what else is happening as long as it's visible and not tawdry.

I think you're also asking about sexual activity, too. Sexual prowess is only important among fairly young people. Sex is much less pivotal later on. My sex drive is lower now, though my erotic imagination is more intense than ever. I've found that my mouth and my hands are as important as my penis in lovemaking now. And as I've said, a back-up young man may sometimes help.

QUESTION: Aside from what you can offer, do you think you are attractive to young women?

CLAUDE: I can enter a room filled with strangers, select the most beautiful young woman there, and leave with her. I can be very charming and intriguing, and my social leverage is substantial. Everything depends on how secure you are within yourself.

QUESTION: Aren't you afraid your young women are after your money?

CLAUDE: That issue can be an element with some women. There may be the dream of an inheritance, but that's not important. Any relationship hinges on the meeting of present and future needs of the partners. The specific nature of those needs, and whether they are all met, may not be important. In my opinion, a May-December relationship can be more stable than the traditional version.

QUESTION: Do you think you will ever marry again?

CLAUDE: No. I learned long ago that marriage is not necessary for a strong relationship. In addition, I have always liked having a wide variety of sexual partners. It took me a long time to find that out.

QUESTION: Has the issue of having a child ever come up with one of your long-term lovers?

CLAUDE: Yes. I'm sterile and I advised her to choose another father or adopt. I saw no problem in my raising a child. She decided not to proceed.

QUESTION: Anything else you want to mention about your style of relationships?

CLAUDE: Everything is exaggerated in a relationship that starts with a large age discrepancy. It's almost at a fantasy level. It's likely there will be more romance, more excitement, more new experiences, more everything. For me, all relationships are built on two critical ingredients—a teacher-student connection, and I must genuinely care for the young woman.

I've had long and short relationships. I let them seek their own length, but those two ingredients were always present. Anything can be used by an insecure person to discredit a relationship.

One last point. Many people have asked me why I don't seek an intellectual equal. What a bore! Can you imagine a love affair in which the partners both know the same things and analyze in the same way?

As we searched for less-frequently occurring age-different couples, in a very natural way we found the homosexual age-different couple. We spoke to them in supportive settings which obscured the fact that they had already overcome at least one barrier—sexual preference.

It was fascinating to learn that although homosexuals challenge social customs in one way, many are trapped in the limitations of agism. "An aging homosexual is a sad thing," many people told us. It became clear that many homosexuals were obsessed with retaining eternal youth for themselves or with trying to capture it in their lovers.

When we interviewed Mark, he spent some time telling the story of "coming out" and declaring his homosexuality; then he shifted gears and told about his first attempt to "come out" and confront agism.

Mark is twenty-five, and through friends he learned about Tim, who lives in a nearby city. Tim is a successful physician, and he owns a large house with many rooms. He rents some of the rooms, and the others are constantly filled by a stream of visitors. Stories were told of his parties, his charm and wit, and his ability to compete in cross-country running—all at age sixty-seven.

By the time he met Tim, Mark's expectations were out of control. He expected a sixty-seven-year-old blend of Paul Newman and Robert Redford—who looked thirty. At the moment of meeting, Mark was stunned to realize what his imagination had done to him. Tim was short, stocky, and bald except for a ring of white hair around his head. Mark said, "I immediately rejected him as a potential lover."

During that evening at Tim's house, Mark learned much more. He watched Tim and saw a relaxed, confident man, able to mix well with other people one third his age. Mark saw no self-pity or fear of being alone. When they talked, Tim said, "I know I'm old. I accept it. I don't think about it much, I just live."

Tim went on to describe his activities as a gay activist, his former marriage, and his three children. Tim spoke of several lovers of all ages—"one lover was too confining."

Mark characterized the evening as "push and pull." "I was very attracted to Tim on some levels, but terribly put off by his age. I couldn't seem to get over the age-difference barrier."

Tim asked Mark to stay with him that night, but Mark made flimsy excuses and they never became lovers. Tim knew age was the problem, but it didn't seem to bother him at all. Mark told us he's still working on the age barrier, and getting better all the time.

We searched for and found a homosexual age-different married couple. Only in this way could we learn the details we wanted. We suspected, and it was confirmed, that the age difference had no unique detectable impact on the formalized relationship. The strengths and weaknesses were typical of any homosexual marriage.

Married homosexuals are a minority in gay society. They are largely invisible, because they are less likely to show up in a psychiatrist's office, and they rarely have encounters with the law. Their stable relationship is usually matched by a stable life-style.

Following is a brief description of the union between Tom and Al, told by Al.

This is the story of the most important relationship of my life. I say that even though we made so many mistakes, and we have not lived happily ever after. Before I met Tom, I had lived for three years with a man twelve years older than I. My separation from Peter was painful. During our last year, Peter's involvement with his business became so intense he had little time or energy for me. We talked about it, but he described himself as "moving into a new phase."

I went away for the summer, and as agreed Peter had moved out of the apartment and out of my life when I returned. The most difficult experience that fall was not having anyone to talk to.

I played the field for a while, but that was depressing for me. I suppose I was looking for someone more permanent when Tom appeared, almost like a gift, in my living room. As a lawyer, I suppose I'm a bit stuffy, but I am more attracted to and get along better with professional men. Tom's well-established dental practice impressed me.

Tom had been brought to my place by an old friend. As the evening progressed and my attraction to Tom grew, during a quiet moment my friend whispered to me, "Take it easy—Tom is over fifty." It seems very silly now to think of being cautioned about a twenty-one-year age difference. It never has, and never will be, a factor.

Tom was standoffish and arrogant, but as I learned later it was only a shield for a vulnerable man. Tom stayed on that evening after the others had left, and we talked. His shield fell away and revealed a gentle, mellow man who knew a great deal about the world.

Tom admits that at the time of our meeting he was becoming a jaded, somewhat cynical, and withdrawn man. I knew a lot about the kind of pressures and problems I'd experienced in my life, and Tom had lived much longer. We had in common all the difficulties of a gay professional—the myriad of short-term sexual relationships, and the longing for stability in our emotional lives.

Perhaps the major difference between us was the ten-year-long alliance with Isaac that Tom experienced. Tom expected the relationship to be endless, and its demise left him unwilling to risk in that way again. That was years ago, but I knew that the memories could mean problems for us.

Tom and I began to be a couple. The beginnings were slow and subtle. As Tom opened to me, I was eagerly ready. Then one lovely Indian summer day, perhaps four months after we met, we were lying in the sun by the pool at Tom's apartment. I was mildly moaning about the distance between our apartments when Tom very matter-of-factly said, "Perhaps we should start looking for a house suitable for the two of us."

Truly being together in our own place took months, but we were a couple, and I loved him.

We slowly introduced each other to our respective circles of friends—gay and straight. There were awkward moments with his sister, my parents, and some of our friends. Most of these scrapes came from issues of homosexuality, not age difference. Occasionally one of our gay friends would make a pass at Tom or me, but only, they confessed later, because they assumed that because of our age difference we were not serious about each other.

We were serious—in fact, we decided to be monogamous. The irritations from the world around us seemed to be never-ending. We purchased a grand condominium, but for appearance's sake put the deed in Tom's name. Officially, I was just a guest. Whenever we spent time with my parents, we chose our words so carefully that when we returned home we collapsed in exhaustion.

Between the two of us, we had enormous amounts of money but were limited in using it according to our wishes. Instead of a full-time housekeeper and the implicit complications of that situation, we settled for twice-a-week visits from a maid. Whenever we had a straight guest we went through the routine of mussing up "Tom's bedroom." We were as open about our love for each other with as many people and situations as possible. However, that did not prevent a steady trickle of hostility from unexpected sources being directed at us. Without even realizing it, we modeled our relationship on a heterosexual marriage. We didn't go through a ceremony like some of our friends, but we considered ourselves married and expected fidelity. The first three or so years flew by. Our professions went well, and we were right for each other. My energy is high and a bit frenetic, but Tom stabilized me. I pepped up some of Tom's old-maidish ways. We balanced each other beautifully, and our lives were very rich.

Somewhere about our fourth year, I had a shock. Gossip came my way which said that Tom had been sleeping with another man. I was crushed and furious. Tom, when I confronted him, was frozen with fear that I would leave him. When I pressed him for an explanation, it became clear that he didn't really know why he had stepped out on me. It took some careful reconstruction and the help of a counselor to get by that rough spot.

The villain was finally detected, and it was me. My legal practice had been too successful, and its demands on my time and energy subtly turned Tom to someone else.

Our harmony was fragile for a while, and although there had been other incidents, we are coming up on our eighth anniversary and "doing great."

You emphasized that you wanted me to stress the impact of our age difference on our marriage. That's very difficult for me to do, simply because the effects of age are so minimal compared to the other forces in our life. And I don't see any special age-difference problems in the future. Of course, I admit that Tom is a very youthful-looking fifty-eight, and in excellent condition—but that's my good fortune.

Our biggest problem is the secrecy which permeates so much of our life. The practical and emotional impact of this is beyond most people's belief. We have been able to create a home life, but its stability is always precarious. The endless precautions against even the most casual visitor damage the morale of our lives.

Another concern is legal, and as a lawyer I understand this very well. If anything were to happen to either of us, the remaining one would have severe problems in recovering his share of jointly owned property.

Because of our "illegitimacy" we must be stronger, wiser, and braver than any other couple. When I think of our different birth dates in this context, I almost laugh. What you call our age-different relationship is simply a trading party. Tom is at a phase in his life that allows him to provide many things I want, and the reverse is also true. It's the most natural thing in the world. I know there are many men of widely varying ages in this world who are capable of meeting my needs. Age is not a factor.

Age-different miscegenation is the theme of the final set of couples. There may be those readers who would scoff at that fancy term, and prefer that an age-different interracial marriage be called "two strikes against them." Simultaneously to vault the barriers of racism and agism does seem complicated.

Beyond doubt, interracial marriages are in many respects like any other marriages: they have the same expectations, are subject to the same fluctuations, involve the same problems of living together, and face the same stresses and the same opportunities as any intimate relationship. We wondered, however, how an age factor, added to all those other matters, would influence things. The answer was not easy to find.

First, interracial couples, on the average, were not available for interview. Second, locating an age-different couple among the interracial couples who were willing to be interviewed severely tested our ingenuity. We were successful; we even located an age-different homosexual interracial couple.

The story which follows presents the trials and tribulations, successes and failures of one age-different interracial couple. Their differences, not only in age and race, are so substantial that they experience the entire range of difficulties any group of couples might encounter. It will be difficult to generalize from their lives, except for a broad hint about the impact of the age factor.

First let's meet Sandy. Born and raised in a white middle-class family in the Midwest, on the surface Sandy's childhood was as normal as apple pie. Look a little closer, and you'll find that she was the strong one in a family that included a distracted father, a weak mother, a sickly younger brother, and a lazy older sister. Sandy was the dynamo that generated the sparks in that family.

She's not beautiful, but has that kind of appearance and presence that keeps your eyes lingering after meeting her. She is short and slim, and has long black hair framing a face with skin so white that her veins almost show through. An introduction to Sandy would be followed by a barrage of questions intended to draw you out. If she became your friend, years later she could recall every detail of conversation you ever had with her.

Involved in many high school actvities, she twirled batons, was president of everything, and gravitated towards the sciences. Sandy had no casual friends, only close ones. She brought then, and brings now, an almost brutal honesty to relationships that frightens the fainthearted away. And, quite unexpectedly, she skillfully and spontaneously uses a four-letter-word vocabulary that makes her friends blush.

After high school, Sandy went to a northeastern university and earned a degree in chemistry. Her life focused on her work and a few close friends. Men sought her out, but for friendship and advice—she remained a virgin.

In the middle 1960s, at the height of the civil rights movement, she went to New York to work on a master's degree in biochemistry. Caught up in the political energy around her, Sandy began working on the political campaigns of black leaders in the city. She decided that assisting more black people to elected office would be her contribution to civil rights. During her campaign efforts she met Rick, a black man twenty-one years her senior. He was to become her husband.

Let's learn something about Rick. A big-city man, he was raised as the middle child of three in a strong family unit in Harlem. His parents had migrated from the South years earlier, and all the children were born in New York. His father worked for years as a janitor in a large office building, and his mother helped out as a part-time maid.

Rick has a million stories about growing up. When he was a young boy, his mother started him attending her Baptist church, but spending all day Sunday inside a building irritated him. When he learned the Catholics spent only an hour, he joined them.

Life in Harlem during the Depression was not easy, but Rick's family unit was strong and stable, and his remarks about those days were positive. World War II was in its frenzy when Rick graduated from high school, and he joined the marines immediately.

Rick says he has spent his life fighting boredom. A tall, slender, but muscular man, he always wanted to be where the action and excitement were, and that's what the marines said they had. He got more than he bargained for.

Sent to a training camp in the South, along with other blacks, Rick was severely mistreated for months. The experience was so negative for him that even now he will not return to the South for any reason.

Innovative and intelligent, Rick managed to leave the horror of the marines behind by arranging a transfer to the army. He was trained for an intelligence job, sent to Europe, and commissioned an officer for battlefield performance he has never discussed.

After the war, Rick returned to New York. Like millions of other veterans of that era, he married, started raising a family, and went to college with the assistance of the government. He did well in sociology, loved and cared for his son and daughter, and, as he says, "fended off the excesses of a demanding wife." And through all of that—he was bored.

He graduated from college, and his uncertainty about what to do with his life was resolved by our involvement in the Korean War. Back in the army, Rick served as an intelligence officer, was captured, and spent seven months in a prison camp. After the war he left the army, but he retains his army reserve commission even today.

Rick returned to a marriage damaged beyond repair. That union ended, and he began a career that combined the preparation of his education, his army intelligence experience, and his endless lust for excitement—Rick joined the New York City Police Department.

Sandy was ten years old when Rick became a New York cop, and he was not to meet her for another dozen years. Those years were good for Rick. Salaries from his police job, the extra security work he always did, and his military reserve pay meant there was always plenty of money, and he lived well. He bought a small apartment building and dedicated the proceeds from that investment to help raise his children. But mostly he lived the life of the streets

—all-night stakeouts, meeting dozens of people every week, and relishing the uncertainty of every moment.

Rick's life was filled with deals, angles, information, and a steady stream of women. He lived very simply, worked hard, and loved the ladies. One woman even joined the police department to be nearer to him.

Life with the police was neither simple nor easy. Rampant politics and barely concealed racism influenced every decision, and Rick's advancement was slow. Many small cities would have welcomed Rick as their police chief, but he preferred to remain a small frog in a big pond.

While not a very political person, Rick knew that relief for his race lay partly in getting more blacks elected to power positions. His network of contacts made him valuable to every candidate's effort, and while working on an election in the mid-1960s, Rick met Sandy.

Their meeting was truly the collision of two different worlds. An older, black, street-wise, cynical New York cop met a young, white, intellectual, idealistic, virgin biochemist. All of that, however, took a back seat to their mutual efforts to help out their candidate. Sandy ran a precinct office, and Rick organized his door-to-door campaign out of that office.

Both Rick and Sandy had recently had disappointing emotional experiences, and were not strongly tied to anyone else. Sandy's blunt honesty and candor literally floored Rick. He claimed that before Sandy "it had been years since I knew a woman who didn't try to manipulate me."

It was as though Sandy were in another culture, with no experience to draw on. Rick wanted to take her out, but he was afraid of her. Eventually they developed a friendship, but though attracted to her, Rick proceeded very slowly.

Rick told me the story of their first real date. "I invited Sandy to my apartment to have dinner with me. I was very nervous, wanted everything to go right, so I cleaned the whole place and prepared a super steak dinner. We finished eating about nine, and Sandy looked at me and blurted, 'Okay, Rick, is that it? Thanks. I've got to get home now.' She left, and that kind of thing went on for months."

After six months of dinners, parties, movies, and Rick trying to put his best foot forward, they became lovers. Rick immediately suggested marriage, but Sandy, who had just begun to work on her doctorate, settled for sharing an apartment.

After a year of living together—a year of Rick worrying about Sandy being labeled as "just another white chick living with a black dude," they married. The ceremony was not memorable—a quick trip to a justice of the peace. Sandy had kept her parents informed of her activities and her relationship with Rick. They never acknowledged his existence. When she called with the news of her marriage, their response was, "Don't come back here anymore."

At this point, Sandy was within a year of completing her doctorate at the university and was working long, hard hours. Rick's police schedule was often unpredictable. Their first year together was chaotic and very difficult for Sandy. Rick missed many meals, came home late, and seemed to be doing dangerous assignments frequently. In restrospect, Sandy admits that underneath her trouble in adjusting to the rhythm of Rick's life was a deep fear of his reputation as a womanizer.

They worked out these issues in the first year. Sandy dealt with her own fears, and Rick was very careful to call and always let her know what was happening. They were being transformed from singles to a married couple.

After the first year, the patterns of their life were formed. Sandy completed her doctorate and dedicated herself to full-time research. Her friends were mostly graduate students from the university. Rick's circle of single "drinking buddies" fell away. Sandy believed that some of these men exploited Rick, and those who were lashed by her sharp tongue did not return.

Sandy told me that through the ups and downs of the first few years, they were always boosted by their incredible sexual compatibility. "Our sex life was and is fantastic," she said.

A small circle of very close friends, mostly white, filled their free hours. Housework was equally divided, and three years slipped quickly away.

Then Sandy developed a new theme. She insisted that because Rick would die so much earlier than she, they must start a family. In this way, "I won't be alone in my old age," she said. This was a curious message from a woman who had spent no time with her own parents since age seventeen.

Rick resisted the idea of another bout of parenting. He'd been through all that before. But as always he deferred to Sandy, and about a year later Andy was born. A hyperactive child, he hit the already chaotic household like a tornado. Rick withdrew, and it became clear to Sandy that raising Andy would be her job.

Four years later, Judy was born. A more placid child, Judy's impact on two overworked people was still substantial.

Now let's bring things up to date. Sandy in her middle thirties and Rick in his middle fifties have been married for eleven years. Andy is eight, and Judy is four. Both parents have two jobs. Sandy has a mild case of the mid-career blues, and Rick is seriously disgruntled about not rising to the professional level appropriate to his capability and qualifications.

Both children have received a great deal of substitute parenting, but are doing well. To compensate for her daytime absences, Sandy has always made a major effort to have special experiences with Andy and Judy during evenings and weekends. Rick's parenting support is mostly indirect. He will take over any chore to leave Sandy free for the kids.

Rick and Sandy have a strong marriage built on a firm foundation, but the children have driven a wedge between them. It's not Rick's age nor his blackness, but probably his natural inclination for a more free-wheeling life-style. Both confessed that they wished "the kids would just grow up and move out."

The age difference betwen Rick and Sandy has never been physically obvious. Rick's appearance has not changed in fifteen years, and some thickening of Sandy's middle has only reduced their "visual age-gap."

Sandy is still an academician, and Rick a street man, but their intellectual powers are not really dissimilar. They just use them in different ways. From soon after their first meeting, Rick wanted a permanent relationship, and that intent has never weakened.

All her life Sandy has been extremely cautious in social-emotional matters. When she relaxed her caution and took Rick as her first man, a powerful bond was established. That bond is still there.

An old acorn suggests that if a married couple has problems, they will be in at least one of three areas: sex, money, or raising the kids. This cliché does not mention age or race, and it may presume a coeval couple.

Nevertheless, in our view of the marriage of Sandy and Rick, neither race nor age appeared to be a factor. They are struggling within the format of a fairly conventional middle-class marriage. If they can continue to adjust its formula to their personal needs, their future together is assured.

Statistically speaking, the odd couples are a tiny minority. We found it fascinating to learn, however, that when these couples are viewed from close quarters, their difficulties are much like those in the majority. The odd couples start from complex social and personal foundations, allow constraints like the age factor to fall away, and strive for happiness like all of us.

CHAPTER SEVEN

Women Are like Fine Wine

Do you know about the double standard of aging? Women have been culturally conditioned to believe that a mature female body is an ugly body. A slightly bulging middle is somehow disgusting for a woman, but a pronounced paunch is an acceptable sign of success for a man. Women have been made to feel that aging is shameful: a disease with no cure, a curse that destroys sexuality, diminishes desirability, and eliminates an active role in the social world.

A new consciousness is changing the minds of many American women. They are realizing that women, like fine wine, improve with age. They are more attractive in maturity than in the awkwardness of youth. These women sense that they are more adept at romance, more stimulating socially, and more free to find love and give it.

Recent statistics, which do not involve well-known people, show that there are two thousand women in this country over fifty-five years of age who are married to men under twenty-five. This is only the tip of the iceberg, because there are many friendships and love relationships in which older women and younger men have successful unions, but these appear in no records.

The social changes of the last decade or two—where did they come from? It's possible that the seed was planted in our society on June 25, 1745 by Benjamin Franklin, when he published his "Advice to a Young Man." Franklin's eight reasons for marrying an older woman have been germinating for over two centuries. The signs of sprouts breaking through the heavy topsoil of social custom are everywhere now, but here are Franklin's words:

1. Because they have more knowledge of the world, and their Minds are better stored with Observations; their Conversation is more improving, and more lastingly agreeable.
2. Because when women cease to be handsome, they study to be good. To maintain their influence over Men, they supply the Diminution of Beauty by an Augmentation of Utility. They learn to do a thousand Services, small and great, and are the most tender and useful of all Friends when you are sick. Thus they continue amiable. And hence there is hardly such a thing to be found as an old Woman who is not a good Woman.
3. Because there is no hazard of children, which irregularly produced may be attended with much inconvenience.
4. Because through more Experience they are more prudent and discreet in conducting an Intrigue to prevent Suspicion. The Commerce with them is therefore safer with regard to your reputation, and with regard to theirs, if the Affair should happen to be known, considerate People might be rather inclined to excuse an old Woman, who would kindly take care of a young Man, form his manners by her good Councils, and prevent his ruining his Health and Fortune among mercenary Prostitutes.
5. Because in every Animal that walks upright, the Deficiency of the Fluids that fill the Muscles appears first in the highest Part. The Face first grows lank and wrinkled; then the Neck; then the Breast and Arms; the lower parts continuing to the last as plump as ever; so that covering all above with a basket, and

regarding only what is below the Girdle, it is impossible of two Women to know an old one from a young one. And as in the Dark all Cats are grey, the Pleasure of Corporal Enjoyment with an old Woman is at least equal and frequently superior; every knack being by Practice capable of improvement.

6. Because the sin is less. The Debauching of a Virgin may be her Ruin, and make her life unhappy.
7. Because the Compunction is less. The having made a young Girl miserable may give you frequent bitter Reflections, none of which can attend making an old Woman happy.

8th and lastly. They are so grateful! [1]

A careful reading of Ben Franklin's axioms, and their implicit sexism, may lead to a bit of queasiness, but the major message is clear. The older woman, fettered for years by bonds she never deserved, deserves to break free.

The cartoonist's stock-in-trade of the short, stocky, overdressed clubwoman has become as outmoded as a corset and pantaloons. No longer are women over forty expected to dress like matrons and concern themselves chiefly with prayers, good works, and the adoration of their grandchildren. These vintage women have better things to do than play bridge, spend hours over a luncheon table worrying about their weight, and discuss their latest hairstyles.

These women are running corporations, selling millions of dollars' worth of real estate, and owning great chunks of the world around us. The old joke about the smart husband who trades in his forty-year-old wife for two twenty-year-old cuties won't get as many laughs any more.

An advice columnist, one of those sage barometers of our society, recently printed a series of letters regarding the mythical attraction of veteran airline pilots to young, beautiful, and nubile stewardesses. A prompt rebuttal came from a senior pilot, who wrote:

Nonsense. How could a pilot in his forties or fifties, earning more than $75,000 a year, be mesmerized by a stew of twenty, however svelte, who constantly pops her bubblegum and whose favorite monotonously repeated expression is, "Like wow, man!" Whatever the young stew has to offer is inconsequential compared to the very real charms of older women who not only are mature, slender, understanding, intelligent, and good conversationalists, but also are extremely skilled in the many and varied delights of the boudoir and who absolutely shun gum.

I found it fascinating to collect material on the woman-older/man-younger topic. Its use as a theme in media has been intensive, but the shift in viewpoint is often startling. Dr. Robert Seidenberg studied the woman-older relationship as it is treated in media and literature, and concluded:

And to further cloud the issue, the theme of older women-younger men liasions has generally had traumatic endings for both the older woman and the young man who loves her, from *Oedipus Rex* to *The Graduate,* as if their authors, unconsciously or not, were sending out early-warning alerts: Beware! Beware! [2]

When Oedipus married his mother, Jocasta, the outcomes were the suicide of Jocasta and the self-blinded exile of Oedipus. In Mozart's *The Marriage of Figaro,* Figaro is saved from having to marry the aged Marcellina when it is discovered that he is her long-lost son. In *Der Rosenkavalier,* Octavian turned from the older Princess von Werdenberg to the younger Sophie. These tragedies were written by men, and the outcomes for older women can be predicted, based on the dominant older-male viewpoint of the time.

In 1969, a real-life tragedy took place in France. When an affair was discovered between Gabrielle Russier, a thirty-two-year-old divorced schoolteacher, and a seventeen-year-old male student, she was fired and sentenced to prison on morals charges. She fought back in the name of love and attempted to marry the young man. Thwarted by opposition from his father, Mme. Russier committed suicide after being imprisoned twice, examined psychiatrically, and threatened with the loss of her two children.

The law used against Mme. Russier was based on "corruption of a minor." Letters she wrote from prison were published in book form, and a movie, *Mourir d'aimer (To Die of Love),* was based on her tragedy. The sexist charges against her made headlines in France for months. Most critics admitted then that if she had been an older man paying for sexual favors from young girls (or boys), nothing would have happened. We may also speculate that the same circumstances occurring today would not have created any furor.

Dr. Seidenberg cited another case history of the same period. It underscores the psychological arrows aimed at women-older age-different relationships a decade ago.

The therapists insisted that such relationships were incestuous —the woman allegedly was seeking to sleep with her son. In this case a husband forced his wife to see a psychiatrist after she became involved with a young man. Seidenberg wrote:

> In the course of eight months he [the psychiatrist] found and imparted to her the infantile derivatives of her present behavior. She was told she could not accept growing old, that she was too narcissistic, and that she had been, alas, taken in by Women's Lib rhetoric. She was reminded that she would bring disgrace to her prominent husband and adolescent boys. Their egos might be shattered by her "acting out." And finally the therapist found that her attraction to the young man was being displaced from her sons, an attraction that was most pathological.[3]

In the interest of fairness, and updating, I asked two therapists to give me opinions of the quoted analysis. Both were sure that, even back then, competing alternative disagnoses were more feasible, and that different analytic models would give other interpretations of her behavior. Their main point, and mine, is that it is ridiculous to label her as "sick" based on that behavior. Such labeling is simply the pressure of social order leaking through in psychoanalytic guise. That pressure is much less today.

The notion that a woman-older/man-younger relationship is incestuous is generally discounted today. Most men would like to forget that they were born out of and nurtured, trained, and taught by women. It's all part of male society's attempt to diminish the power and authority women have.

The male author's support of the double standard of aging is never more apparent than in Lawrence Durrell's *Mountolive*. Mountolive, an Englishman, has a passionate affair with Leila, the wife of a wealthy Egyptian. They meet again, years later, and each is eager to resume their liaison. Mountolive, shocked at the impact of the years, sees Leila as "a fattish Egyptian lady with all the marks of eccentricity and age written upon her appearance." On the other hand, Leila says to Mountolive, "You have not changed by a day."

Plays and films come in for their share of the older-woman/younger-man theme. In *Tea and Sympathy,* a young man is rescued from homosexuality and isolation in a hostile environment when the wife of his headmaster gives him intellectual and sexual solace. This is the older woman in her role as nurse. A love relationship between an adolescent boy and a beautiful, thirtyish woman is portrayed in *Cold Wind in August.* In the fall, when the boy is to leave to begin college, the woman takes a job as a stripper and makes sure her lover sees her performance. Here the older woman is portrayed as evil. In *The Lovers,* the bored and nonorgasmic wife of a rich industrialist begins a love affair with a young pauper. Her response is marvelous, but she refuses to run away with the youth because of her children. Joe Lampton, in the movie *Room at the Top,* leaves a deep love affair with an older, poor woman in order to marry a very rich young woman whom he does not love. The age-different theme in each of these older movies is overlaid with the message that love is secondary to other considerations. Money, career, and filial development push love aside in the scramble for priority.

A review of more recent films using the woman-older/man-younger theme also leaves me uneasy. The movie version of Stephen Vizinczey's *In Praise of Older Women* defined an older woman as, say, thirty-five, but the couples in the film looked more coeval than age different. If the presentation had used forty-year-old women who looked forty (instead of thirty-five-year-olds who looked twenty-five), the admission-paying public might have balked.

The reviews of *Moment by Moment,* the love story of a beach bum and a rich Beverly Hills housewife that starred Lily Tomlin and John Travolta, were so poor that any message promoted by the film is likely to suffer. In *Players,* the younger man persists and eventually wins the older woman, but the principals, particularly the older woman, are presented as such tarnished characters that there is little potential joy in the union. The viewer is only glad they finally get together, and wishes that they would go away.

In my judgment, the most recent insightful treatment of the age-different theme (even though it's man-older) was by Woody

Allen in *Manhattan*. The protagonists, a forty-two-year-old writer —who is appropriately saggy and cynical—and a seventeen-year-old high school student with a little squeaky voice, have a wonderfully tender and mature love affair. He drops her for an opportunity with a coeval lover. Later, when his older lover abandons him, he returns to his teenage lover to ask forgiveness. For the first time in a film, the romantic power of the man-older/woman-younger couple is acknowledged in a realistic fashion.

Underlying every movie I've mentioned is the basic commercial appeal—sexual titillation. Make no mistake about it. The image of a young male body and an older female body entwined in love-making is what keeps the cash registers ringing. The filmmakers are capitalizing on the kind of feelings I described about Mrs. Macintosh in chapter 1. Only nowadays the man-older couple is no longer sufficiently exciting.

The most powerful example of the intense sexual energy generated by the woman-older/man-younger couple was depicted in an early 1970s film, *Summer of '42*. Picture the scene. A beautiful woman of twenty-two lives in a cottage on an ocean beach and awaits the return of her husband from World War II. She develops a friendship with a fifteen-year-old boy in the nearby town. On the night she receives word of her husband's death, in a scene uniquely blending tears and desire, she makes love to the boy.

While the waves pounded the beach and clouds flew by the moon, the boy and the woman came together in a sexual act a psychistrist would call *eros*—the imperative that life and union must be sustained. A newspaper movie reviewer of that time said:

> The lovemaking scene, a mix of teary faces and bare shoulders, was the most erotic scene I have ever seen, and was unhealthy for young people because of the seven-year age difference of the participants.

The woman-older/man-younger love union still confronts a rather strong social taboo, and that sells tickets to movies. Toni Tucci calls it "the last taboo." Her book, *The Butterfly Secret,* is about the man-younger match and has sold 500,000 copies. Jane Seskin and Bette Ziegler take a journalistic look at these couples in *Older Women/Younger Men.*

A few of the famous who love to ignore taboos are: Ruth Gordon, eighty-two, and Garson Kanin, sixty-six; Merle Oberon, sixty-six, and Robert Wolders, forty; Gloria Swanson, eighty, and William Dufty, sixty-three; Sybil Burton, fifty, and Jordon Christopher, thirty-eight; and Dr. Phyllis Chesler, thirty-eight, and Nachmy Bronstein, a twenty-eight-year-old premedical student.

These couples are married. Some of the unmarried twosomes include: Dyan Cannon, forty, and actor Armand Assante, twenty-nine; Louise Fletcher, forty-four, and James Mason's twenty-three-year-old son Morgan; Ellen Burstyn, forty-six, and the twenty-seven-year-old painter Michael Davidson; and Georgia O'Keeffe, ninety-one, and potter Juan Hamilton, thirty-three.

The qualities these couples seek are summarized by Erica Jong.

It's the solution to a lot of women's problems these days. Younger men generally take an egalitarian relationship for granted. It's no big accomplishment for them to share the housework and the child care—things that would have been unheard of in their father's generation.[4]

A recent *New York Times* article quoted a thirty-three-year-old Manhattan businesswoman who is married to a man six years younger.

Once you're liberated you start to feel just like a man looking at a multitude of nubile young things. You start to think, "Who wants a wrinkled, flabby, potbellied 40 or 50 year old man when you can have one who is young and firm." It makes you feel so much better about your own body.[5]

Other couples cite the very practical fact that since so many coeval marriages fail, how could an age-different match fare any worse?

Francine du Plessix Gray, writing in the book review section of the *New York Times* and discussing Collette's novel *Chéri*, made a crucial point:

What Lea treasures the most in her young lover is "the trust, the relaxation, the avowals, the sincerity, the indiscreet expansion, that quasifilial gratitude which an adolescent pours without restraint at the breast of a warm and mature friend." The perfect balance of Lea and Chéri's liaison is not so much based on ideal sensuous mating as on that precious self-image —the bulwark of all life-giving relationships—which they offer each other.

Ms. Gray goes on to say:

> Only a deeply feminized society such as France, where the prestigious civilizing power of older woman has been deeply rooted since the 16th century in the tradition of the *salons,* could nurture a creative vision of this particular form of bonding.[6]

Let's take a look at the "creative vision" of a typical middle-class American couple. Recently, Ken and Jean celebrated their tenth wedding anniversary. Ken is thirty and Jean is forty-three. Jesalee and I talked to them a few days after their anniversary party, and Jean was still getting used to wearing her new gold-link bracelet from Ken. While the four of us were getting comfortable together before beginning the interview, Ken commented that a large framed and engraved apology would also be an appropriate gift. He went on to say that his half-baked attitude towards their age difference nearly scuttled their marital ship many times. Ken's story turned out to be the one we wanted, and here are his own words.

When I said I owed many apologies to Jean, I was referring to one of the most important things I learned after meeting her. I had answered for myself every question I thought I had about our difference in ages before I asked Jean to marry me. What I forgot was that no matter how hard you try to turn away from stupid, irrational prejudices, they are not really destroyed. They are still around waiting to gum up the works when you are angry or mean enough to call on them.

I met Jean when I was on vacation in Florida. I love those miles and miles of white sand beaches. I spent hours walking and collecting shells. One afternoon, I was drifting along a remote section of beach, when I saw someone approaching from the opposite direction. Eventually, I could see it was a woman with a collecting bag like mine slung over her shoulder. As we drew closer, I saw that she was beautiful and wearing a bright red bikini.

Comparing our shells was the most natural thing in the world, and we beachcombed together for several days after our chance meeting. Her company was wonderful, and when her vacation ended, and she was about to leave, I asked for her address.

I'll never forget that moment. She turned to me and said, "How old are you?"

I said, "I'm twenty."

She said, "I'm thirty-three."

I admit I was shocked speechless. I hadn't even thought about her age. Finally I muttered, "So what?" but strange feelings were sweeping over me. I was so attracted to Jean, but as we stood talking, a kind of confusion blurred my thoughts. I bluffed my way through that scene, and later we started visiting each other on weekends.

I learned that Jean was a widow. Her husband had drowned in a boating accident five years before we met. I saw pictures of him, and he looked handsome, sophisticated, and older. Apparently their marriage was not a good one. He didn't want children, and Jean suspected he ran around with other women.

In no time at all, I was in love with Jean. Some friends thought I was absolutely crazy, and others envied me because of Jean's presumed sexual prowess. Both viewpoints upset me. Most of my buddies were marrying their high school sweethearts.

My mother assumed I'd been hooked by a smart opportunist. "A widow and thirteen years older! Are you out of your mind? She must think we're rich. There's got to be something the matter with her, or she'd get a husband her own age."

My parents continued zapping me with their bad feelings about Jean. I hoped that when they met her, their resistance would melt, but her first visit was a horror. First, my mother

cornered me and insisted that our family doctor was pretty
sure Jean was too old to start having children. Then my
father took me aside, and made the dire prediction that when
I was "feisty in my forties" Jean would be over the hill.
To top it all, my older brother and his wife intimated to
Jean that it was her sexual experience that allowed her to
capture me. All in all, the meeting was a bummer. But
through the visit, Jean was calm and gracious, and afterward
I knew that nothing had changed for us.

A few months later we were married, and spent two idyllic
honeymoon weeks in our isolated mountain cabin. Our
lovemaking had always been good, but after our marriage
we came together in such an intense union, I can't properly
describe it. I returned to work absolutely certain I had
done the right thing.

We both wanted children, and within a few months Jean
was pregnant. Her obstetrician scoffed at the possibility of
trouble, and Jimmy was born with no problems. In a little
over a year, Tommy made the fourth in our family. The
two little boys melted my mother a lot, but she still put her
claws in Jean every now and then. Once, soon after Tommy
was born, when she saw Jean doing exercises, she said,
"Don't bother—at thirty-five your muscles will never snap
back."

In a short while, however, Jean was as slim and beautiful
as ever. Life was very rich for me through those years.
My father's construction business was doing well, and I was
steadily being given more responsibility. Jean was a super
mother. Perhaps it was her maturity, but she was even-tempered
and careful, and dealt with a million minor emergencies
without the chaos I saw in other families.

The years flew by, and when I raised my head to look
around, the boys were both in school, and Jean had just
turned forty. Something started happening. The early scrambling
at work had passed, and my job was stable. Jean had more
time available now, and we decided to begin having more
social life. We'd kept pretty much to ourselves, so we began
to make more of an effort to develop friendships. The other
couples in the neighborhood were mostly near my age,

with kids that went to school with Jimmy and Tommy.

During our bridge parties and barbecues, for the first time, I started to sense a difference between Jean and the other wives. It wasn't looks—more like a subtlety of behavior— and I thought others were sensing it too.

Quite by accident, I let it slip to one of the husbands that Jean and I had a thirteen-year age difference. Soon, of course, everyone knew, and in small ways they started to treat Jean differently—like not letting her help with the dishes, or not horsing around as much when she was near. The women always seemed to be asking her for advice. The men stopped flirting and seemed more respectful. Instead of banter, they asked more serious questions such as some issue the P.T.A. might be concerned about.

The changes toward Jean bothered me. When they treated her like a visiting school teacher, I was somehow resentful. Once a neighborhood girl took a tumble on her bike in front of our house and skinned both her knees. I carried her screaming into our house to tend to her scrapes, and she blurted out, "I don't want you! I want your mother!"

Of course I knew the child was nearly hysterical and probably wanted her mother, or at least some motherly person, but Jean was standing there and heard the little girl's screams. I saw tears streaming down Jean's face, and she seemed to clutch at the streaks of gray in her hair.

That did it. I figured it was time for us to talk about getting older. I didn't know what to say or ask for, but I tried to explain some of the things I'd been feeling. Jean just listened. A few days later she turned up with her natural hair color restored and not a gray hair in sight. She was extra careful after that to wear youthful clothes, and although I liked what I saw, I remained uneasy.

A year and one-half later my father died, and my mother came to live with us. Even though we had been married over eight years then, my mother never truly accepted Jean. My mother took every opportunity to allude to Jean's age or to put her down in some way.

My mother's cracks against Jean seemed to poison my mind, and when Jean and I had an ordinary spat, I found myself being sarcastic about her age. Things got worse and finally Jean struck back. She accused me of being a momma's boy. She said I regretted marrying her. She said she knew I loved her, but that I was getting very confused about what I wanted from her. I had to admit to myself that Jean was right.

It was painfully clear that I was in trouble and needed help. During a regularly scheduled physical exam with the elderly doctor who delivered me, my worries came flooding out. I told him of the unrelenting antagonism of my mother, of my quarrels with Jean, and about my secret fear that our age difference would eventually overcome Jean and me. I confessed that I was beginning to believe that anybody was a fool to buck the age factor.

My wise old friend didn't take long to diagnose my marriage problems. First, he asked me what my mother thought of my girlfriends before Jean, and when I remembered that she hadn't liked any of them, he said, "It's clear to me that your mother's possessiveness would have blocked acceptance of anyone you married."

After we talked some more, the doctor said he had a theory about Jean and me, and he wanted me to think about it. He claimed that I married Jean because of our age difference, not in spite of it. His idea really astonished me. Then he pointed out how I'd gone home after meeting Jean and made a big deal of telling everyone about her age. "You announced it to your family as though you'd committed some kind of a sin," he said. He went on to say that I continued confessing the age difference to my friends as though I had to do penance. He concluded, "Jean is an attractive, youthful woman, and I honestly don't understand what you're fussing about."

I went home dazed. It took a while and it wasn't easy, but I finally had to admit the doctor was right. I had paraded Jean, her age and experience, like a conquest. I wanted to show my family that I was going to marry anyone I wanted. And I wanted my friends to envy me. I'd achieved everything I seemed to need, only I was the last one to realize it.

My long-delayed insight that Jean and I are uniquely right for each other changed my life. No, not really—it changed my attitude. During the past two years, the little situations that used to bug me just haven't happened. I guess it was all in my mind. I had a kind of sensitivity that caused me to overreact to everything.

When I let my self-doubt go, I realized that the problems of my marriage were no different from those of anyone else. In fact, I suspect my situation is better than most. I've read that women often remain sexually vigorous longer than men, so Jean and I will balance better. Women live longer, too, so that means we have the opportunity of being together our entire lives. No long widowhood for Jean.

The plaque I should give Jean on our tenth anniversary must have our family motto: Age doesn't make any difference.

As we sought women-older age-different couples, and talked to many people, we kept hearing a sentence repeated: "I felt liberated and wanted to experiment." The women who spoke this sentence were usually talking about short-term relationships. Among a certain group of women, having an affair with a young man has become one of the rites of passage to a new kind of freedom. Suzanne, thirty-eight, is such a woman.

My first affair with a young man was quite by accident. I had been working seventy-hour weeks for over a month, and I was exhausted. I took a week of vacation and headed for a friend's mountain cabin for a week of sun and solitude. I figured fresh air and the simple life would speed my recovery. Wires got crossed, however, and on the second day my friend's eighteen-year-old brother turned up expecting to use the cabin.

Familiar to me from the past as an annoying adolescent, Tom had become a handsome young man. At first it seemed like he had come back to continue his annoyances, but we talked over our timing conflict, and he agreed to use the sofa in the living room and stay out of my hair.

Our coexistence worked for a couple of days. My tan was developing, and the sharp edges on my personality were rounding off a bit. Once, I saw Tom walk naked out of the lake after a swim, and I felt a stirring in my own body. "Come on," I said to myself, "he's your friend's kid brother."

Early in the morning of the third day, I passed through the

living room on my way to the lake. Tom, still asleep on the sofa, lay sprawled without a stitch of clothing. Without meaning to, I paused and just looked at him. I don't know how long I stood there—probably less than a minute—when suddenly his eyes opened. Neither of us moved for a few moments, then I continued out the door.

Somehow, in those few seconds of eye contact, everything changed. We chatted briefly several times during the day, and then rode bikes to the grocery store for food and an agreed upon cooperative dinner.

Tom was fun. He treated me in a casual, playful way I hadn't experienced for years. I prepared the chicken and Tom built the salad, then we laughed through the entire meal. I had begun to think of him as a sexy man, and fantasies were churning through my mind.

After dinner we sipped wine in front of the fireplace. My maternal admiration for Tom dwindled and was replaced by a growing lust. I knew that Tom would not make a sexual move towards me, possibly even with my encouragement. We had too many years of playing other roles with each other to change so easily.

I worried about Tom's sister, my dear friend, and their parents. "What will they all think?" rumbled through my mind. Losing Tom by making a wrong move was also in my fantasies. The cost of seducing Tom seemed very high.

While these thoughts muddied my mind, Tom went on chatting, quite unaware of my ruminations. Evening came, and the cabin was lighted only by the flames of our small fire. I knew we had reached some kind of turning point. The question was—what next?

Without ever deciding to, I stood up, slipped out of my clothes in a moment, and stood there in the firelight. Tom looked at me for a long time. Slowly and deliberately, he stood, and seconds later he was naked beside me. Without speaking, I took his hand and led him to the bedroom. We were stupendous together. Through a long night of lovemaking, we never spoke.

I'd forgotten how exciting an open, uninhibited young man who loved sex and women could be. I'd also forgotten the inexhaustible energy of a young man. Though he was far from an expert lover, his enthusiasm and energy more than compensated. Tom tried everything on me, and if something didn't work, he didn't seem to mind.

The rest of the week was a dream. We didn't change towards each other. We still had the good vibes for each other that we'd had through the years. We just added sex.

We never spoke of the future, and at week's end we kissed goodbye and went on with our separate lives. No one ever knew about our affair. Whenever we see each other, we are affectionate and friendly as we always were. During special moments Tom has winked at me or patted my fanny, but we never had sex again.

Tom gave me an invaluable gift. He helped me over an enormous emotional barrier by being my first young lover.

I've spent time with several young men since then, and I've learned that the relationship that develops between us has little to do with our ages.

Suzanne experienced the self-doubt that may accompany an age-different union. She dealt with it by keeping it a secret, at least the first time. Helen Van Slyke has said of this problem:

How often does she [an older woman] leave her equal-age husband for a man young enough to be her son? . . . how likely is she to marry, form a liaison with or even date someone considerably her junior. Not likely. Years of conditioning have produced a female belief that there is something wrong with the woman who's older than her man. Or something wrong with him. She's been trained to believe that becoming involved or even being seen with a man ten or fifteen years younger than herself (not to mention twenty-five or thirty!) makes her instantly suspect. At best she's made to feel ridiculous. At worst, she's a cradle snatcher, a desperate old fool who can attract only homosexuals or fortune hunters. In the eyes of the world she is—sin of all sins—a woman who doesn't act her age.[7]

Another part of growing up female in our culture is the ritual of age deception. Gender, for many women, creates a certain kind of liar. Birthdays become a dreaded experience. Some women avoid aging by mounting and maintaining a campaign of trickery. For others there is merely an apologetic evasiveness about age.

The double standard of aging, and its impact on relationships, is so absurd. More women over forty are now facing their middle years with confidence. Their theme is: "You're not getting older, you're getting better."

Verta Mae Smart-Grosvenor quotes her Cousin Flossie: "A woman who will tell her age will tell anything." Flossie never seemed to change as she aged. When asked about it, she said, "If you tell folks how old you are and you look good, folks will talk about you like a dog around other people. And if you don't look good and tell, they talk about you like a dog. So a woman over forty should never tell her age." [8]

The "can't win for losing" attitude of an elderly middle-class woman is being shed by later generations. Rose is an example. However, for an overweight, over-forty vice-president of a small midwestern bank to shed old conditioning, a new set of problems must be managed. Here is Rose's story.

I admit it. I really enjoy the college-age man. Often, however, they don't know how to behave, and they have no sense of the appropriateness of things. I'm forty-five, fifteen pounds overweight, and I have to wear business-type clothing nearly all the time. I try to present a serious and responsible facade all the time. The first young man I dated worked at the bank, and that affair never got off the ground. The gossip was intolerable, and I dropped him.

I met my next young fellow in a restaurant. He was well dressed and well behaved, and I was so impressed I went home with him. I was very afraid of going to his apartment, and it turned out I had a right to be. Drugs were his thing, and I ran, not walked, to the nearest exit. Before I could get away, however, I had a black eye as a memento.

That experience kept me at home for a while, but after a while I convinced myself that it was just a fluke. An older man might have been an alcoholic, and hitting a woman is more accepted in some cultures.

The next young guy was Ted. He was your typical starving artist, and after we had gone out a few times—all of a sudden he was living with me. For a while it worked. He painted all day while I was at the bank. Other than a few derisive cracks about the "world of finance," we got along fine. He was fabulous in bed.

One morning after about two months, we got into a terrible battle. It started simply enough. Ted needed my car to pick up some supplies, and he asked me to take the bus to work. Sometimes I did that, but on this particular day I had a business meeting across town, and I needed the car. We tried to negotiate the problem, but everything got out of hand. In the midst of screaming at each other about whose work was more important, he grabbed my car keys and wouldn't give them back. In desperation I ran to the bus stop, and barely caught the last bus that would get me to the bank on time.

About midmorning Ted stalked into the bank. He planted himself in front of my desk and started shouting crazy things about poor people and ripoffs. I was petrified. I've worked long and hard for many years in order to get to my current position, and I'm not about to sacrifice it for some phony liberal.

Somehow, I'll never know how, I got Ted out of the bank, and then it took my lawyer over a week to get him out of my house. When I left the hotel where I'd been staying and went home, I found that Ted had left a disaster area. He wrecked the place.

That did it. I was so distraught I wound up seeing a therapist to try to figure out what was happening in my life. I love the vitality and sexual energy of a young man, and my therapist tried to convince me that I just didn't know how to pick one. Maybe he's right, but I'm afraid to try again. Right now I'm dating a thirty-four-year-old married man. I don't see him too often, but the relationship is safe and easy.

The male position in the woman-older/man-younger couple is aptly described by Langston Hughes in "Preference."

> I likes a woman
> Six or eight and ten years older'n myself.
> I don't fool with these young girls.
> Young girl'll say,

> Daddy, I want so-and-so.
> I needs this, that, and the other.
> But an old woman'll say,
>   Honey, what does YOU need?
>   I just drawed my money tonight
>   and it's all your'n.
> That's why I likes an older woman
> Who can appreciate me:
> When she conversations you
> it ain't forever, Gimme! [9]

A crass view, of course, but nevertheless an element of what some young men told us. Take Dick, for example. Dick describes his wife, Mary, in this way. "She takes care of things. No matter how much chaos or trouble occurs, Mary can handle it." Dick is twenty-eight and Mary is forty-four. They have worked together for several years in Dick's small importing business.

Dick was in his early twenties when his father turned over the business. Dick had a young wife and two tiny children, and the combination was too much for him. His marriage failed, but the business survived—only because Mary came to work for him.

Mary did everything. No job was too big or two small. She sorted out customs and shipping problems, advised customers, and helped acquire merchandise. The hours required never made any difference. After she and Dick were married, she helped with his children, his weak ex-wife, and his invalid mother.

Mary is not a fool or a workaholic. She is a strong, organized, and mature woman with a deep sense of her own capability. She loves Dick and has a graceful way of getting done what needs to be done.

Alex is the soldier-of-fortune type. He came from a very political family with plenty of money on his mother's side. After a posh education he dallied through several business ventures and then drifted into the army. He was very dashing as an officer and always sought difficult and dangerous assignments.

At thirty, Alex married a fifty-year-old, once-beautiful woman, with whom he lived in violence and drama. Their life together was a series of skirmishes embedded in a major battle. Neither ever seemed to tire of the endless hassling. Some of us speculated that Alex married a cold older woman to act out his deep anger towards his always-bitchy mother.

Who knows? Whatever they wanted, they both got. Their marriage endures, and one can only assume a set of mutual needs is being met.

Our society has a complex version of a sexual double standard. Men have always received society's permission to be more active sexually in their teens, while women were supposed to be virgins. A version of this code exists among oldsters. Older men play around, but older women don't. And the curious paradox overlying these standards is that the "sexual prime" theory suggests that women in their early forties and boys in their late teens are at their sexual peaks.

Old codes are crumbling, and sensual older women seek sexy young men for love affairs. The surface reasons for these connections vary, but underneath is pure sex. Leona is an example. She is a forty-five-year-old suburban housewife, her children are grown and gone, her husband travels frequently, and her life is filled with projects. Some projects are political, some are charitable, and one is sexual.

Al is Leona's sexual project. They met when he applied for a part-time gardening job. The moment she saw him, Leona knew Al was a diamond in the rough. He was twenty, handsome, and used to living by his wits. But Al had no wisdom about how to earn a living in any orthodox way. Leona promptly became Al's teacher. She set him up in a small apartment near her home and began to teach him gardening. Not just mowing the lawn, but pruning, potting, and all the fancy things she did in her greenhouse in the back yard. Then she taught Al how to drive, how to cook, and how to be a butler. She even showed him money management and got him involved in some small investments.

And while all the teaching and learning was going on, Leona and Al were lovers. They had sex at every time of the day or night, in every way, and in every location one could imagine. Al was her stud, and Leona was his mentor. The exchange pleased both of them for over three years. Finally, Al drifted into other successes, and Leona continues to find young sex partners in ways that are comfortable for her.

Training a young man in the ways of the world is attractive to many older women. It's an effort not unlike the ancient customs practiced by all the courtesans of history. A charming reverse version of this was practiced by Kathy and Todd.

Kathy, at forty-three, divorced her husband and found herself in a very unfamiliar singles scene. Twenty years of marriage and a successful career as an accountant did not prepare her for a social world that had rushed on and left her behind. Meeting Todd, twenty-two, changed all that.

Todd and his father ran a small restaurant near Kathy's office. Kathy lunched there sometimes and knew Todd only as a handsome young figure in the background of a busy noon rush.

Kathy changed when she became a single woman, and Todd noted the difference and the missing wedding rings. One noon, quite candidly, Todd asked if he could see her socially, and before Kathy knew it she had agreed to meet him for dinner.

With the noisy lunch crowd gone, Todd's restaurant by candlelight became a romantic bistro. Todd was charming. Instinctively, he was sympathetic when Kathy told him of her recent divorce. Most other people gave her personal upheaval a ho-hum. When they discussed their hobbies and interests, Kathy was instantly aware that Todd was involved in the latest things that she knew nothing about. Later, when Todd took Kathy home, there was no sexual pressure. It was clear to Kathy that Todd was special.

Todd began to call Kathy regularly for dates. The first was a short motorcycle trip up the coast to visit a special restaurant. Kathy found her first ride on a motorcycle a blend of terror and delight. Then there were horseback riding and backpacking trips into remote wilderness areas. Their first lovemaking happened by a mountain lake.

Todd showed Kathy a new world. She began to appreciate the outdoors as something different from what she passed through on the way to work. New music and ideas became available to her. Even her clothing changed to brighter colors and softer lines. And always there was the lovemaking. As much as she wanted—any time she wanted.

There were a few embarrassing moments for Kathy. Sometimes the quizzical glances of strangers made her uneasy with Todd. And sometimes Todd's friends were hard to talk to. Neither she nor

Todd ever mentioned love. A part of Kathy wondered how she could have such experiences with Todd and never mention love.

Ultimately, love was their undoing, only not in the way Kathy expected. One day, after nearly two years of dating, Todd came to Kathy and told her he had fallen in love. It turned out to be a love-at-first-sight episode with a new acquaintance his age. With little warning, Todd was gone.

But the student no longer needed the teacher. Kathy was in a new world and doing well. Her last words to us were, "Every day I learn something new."

The newer verision of "She's young enough to be your daughter" is "He's young enough to be your son." That, of course, is the snide remark often aimed at the older-woman member of an age-different couple. The incestuous overtones of the intended put-down blur the fact that the generation gap is not very wide. And the older one gets, the shorter the gap appears.

Many women, however, have painful emotional reactions when they have to confront the fact that their lovers could, at least chronologically, be their sons. One woman told us that she became nauseated and had to leave the room whenever a friend made that wounding accusation to her.

Where is the power in that silly chronological comparison? I'm sure Ed in chapter 2 would just yawn if we insist that Lou is young enough to be his granddaughter. My theory is that a person who is bothered by that sort of chronological comment is likely to be caught in a general agism problem.

Think about it. If that agism assertion bothers you, it's likely that you discriminate against people, based on age, in others parts of your life. How many close friends do you have who are twenty years older or younger than you? If you are a person who never thinks much about age, your own or anyone else's, then age-different alliances are a natural for you.

One interviewee told us that before she shed her agism limitations, she vacillated between being her young man's insatiable wild lover and his mother. After a long night of torrid lovemaking, sometimes she was tempted to get out of bed and ask if he wanted a glass of milk. She offered her young lover a confusing blend of eroticism and maternalism.

An interesting variation on the age-different sensitivity problem occurs when the age difference is not so marked. Men and women lie about their ages enough in order to appear more credible to each other. The necessary adjustment of birthdays, anniversaries, and temporal memories of all kinds is complicated.

Dee's story is an example of age-different confusion. She is a beautiful forty-year-old woman who buys jewelry for a large department store. She is well educated, moves in fairly sophisticated circles, and takes excellent care of herself. Her weekly routine includes exercise classes, careful eating habits, and the willingness to take time to follow the guidance of a skin specialist.

Recently Dee met Larry when he became the buyer for men's clothing. She told him she was thirty, and later, when it turned out Larry was thirty-two, that seemed just right. Dee and Larry started going out, and a romance soon developed.

It didn't take Dee long to realize the sticky position she was in. First, she had to make sure Larry didn't meet any of her old friends or relatives who might give her age away. She constantly had to remember what she was doing ten years ago and then imagine what she might have been doing if she were actually a decade younger. Even in light conversation the pressure on her was unbearable.

Eventually, of course, an uncensored remark did give Dee away. One day when they were remembering favorite movies, and old titles were flitting through their conversation, Dee mused that she had seen *Shane* when she was in college. Something flashed in Larry's mind, and later when he checked he learned that *Shane* came out when he was in the fifth grade.

That slip did it. Larry was furious at having been deceived by Dee, broke off with her, and hasn't spoken to her since. But Larry's exodus probably saved Dee's sanity. Dee sometimes speculates that if she had been honest, her age wouldn't have made any difference.

Elsa is much more pragmatic about the age factor. She says, "Either you look your age or you don't. Either they like you as you are or they don't. If being interested in younger men inspires you to go from size 16 to size 10 or to work out at a gym, fine. As long as you don't think you're fooling anybody and don't make an ass of yourself."

We asked several middle-aged women about their efforts to remain young enough looking to be attractive to young men. Their answers were a very mixed bag. Some of the approaches were physical. Beyond exercise and diet was everything the cosmetic industry had to offer—and beyond that were the surgical tricks. One woman said, "Anything that enables you to go out and do battle in a cold and inhospitable world, whether it's coloring the gray in your hair or major surgery—as long as you don't try to achieve the impossible—has to be a plus."

Other women took the inner approach to improvement. They worked on their attitudes and their emotional limitations. They admitted that if they were genuinely attracted to younger men and if they planned to act on that attraction, self-doubt and a social stigma were waiting around the corner. So by a variety of self-improvement methods they strengthened the maturity that helped make them attractive to young men.

CHAPTER EIGHT

My Dear Friend

THE MOST HOLY bond of society is friendship," wrote Mary Wollstonecraft, the eighteenth-century English writer. This powerful statement only begins to reveal the importance of friendship. The search for simple human affection is a significant effort in most lives. Previous times and places are valued according to the quality of attachments.

This book is about enriching your life. There is no greater opportunity for enrichment than that offered by a nurturing network of friendships. Harvey Cox, writing about the millions of young Americans who have become involved in new spiritual movements, says, "Most of the members of these movements seem to be looking for simple human friendship." [1]

"Stop!" you may be thinking. Supporting friendship is like taking a stand for motherhood. Not so—not in our society. Marriage, parenthood, and work are obligatory social roles that give meaning and purpose to adulthood. Friendship, on the other hand, is an optional social role. Almost everyone in our culture agrees it is good to have friends, but it is not necessary, or even considered appropriate, to invest the amount of time and energy in friendships that one devotes to family responsibilities and work. Societal judgment of our success as adults rests primarily on our success in our family and work, not on the number or quality of friendships we have.

Other factors complicate friendships for us. Christianity, by definition, says we are all brothers. The church is jealous of any relationship that prevents an individual from devoting all of his love to God. Our democratic form of society stresses free individuals—standing alone.

Friends are often little more than business acquaintances contacted with commercial intent. Our mobile society, where cross-country moves are routine, forces us periodically to reconstruct our set of friends completely. For some, excessive interest in nurturing friendships is taken as a sign of weakness in a society that stresses competition and self-interest.

Many Americans use relatives, even extremely distant ones, as friends. Robert Brain touches a major influence when he writes:

> Modern marriage, based on romantic love, has been described as one of Western civilization's greatest inventions, with its combination of romantic passion, loving friendship, sex, and ceremonial union between a man and a woman. The love of a husband and wife in our society is a remarkable fusion of sex, domesticity, and comradeship. It is also self-sufficient: in theory, neither partner needs emotional satisfaction outside the warm walls of the family. This is a unique and perhaps dangerous situation. No other society, as far as I know, attempts to satisfy all the emotional needs of two persons within such a restricted framework.[2]

It is important that, before we move on to age-different friendships, we understand the contradictions about friendship in our society. Other cultures have rich and varied traditions of friendship, but we do not. Nearly everyone applauds the idea of friends, but we expect friendship to survive based on the vague bonds of moral sentiment. It has no ceremonies or traditions and few expectations. Friendship has the potential of meeting a social need. All our contacts spoke of wanting a strong emotional tie to other people— not based on sex or the social arrangements of marriage.

Social scientists have largely ignored the conceptual study of friendship. A few have taken data and reported on how friendships form. Two obvious major critical factors are proximity and similarity. First, we must know the other person exists, and then have a basis to make contact. Nearly everyone has sensed that around the corner, or across town or somewhere, there are people who would make wonderful friends. But how do we find them?

The isolation of modern life makes the location of a mate or a friend incredibly complex. Some use computers and astrological predictions to identify appropriate mates. Prearranged friendships would help overcome the enormous requirement of proximity.

Once contact is made, a common way of selecting friends is to choose "people like me." In effect, many people carry around very specific constraints on the acceptability of friends. These limitations may include sexual, economic, religious, racial, social, geographic, physical, and other factors. Frequently, there is an age factor.

The romantics of our culture condemn the arranged marriages of other cultures. Erich Fromm reassured us over twenty years ago that the act of loving is what is important and not the target of the love. With appropriate will and commitment present, Fromm says, it doesn't much matter who your mate is.

It's like that in friendship. Being friendly and loving enriches our lives, and there need be no set of requirements any friend must meet.

For most people the emotional hierarchy runs something like this. The primary love relationship comes first. When there is plenty of love, followed by satisfactory work, in an individual's life, the needs for friendship may be very low. However, if there is a change in social activity or in roles, the emotional need for friends may skyrocket.

Take the elderly, for example. They need friends to soften the impact of retirement or widowhood. However, just when friendship becomes most important, friendship opportunities are fewer than ever before. The loss of work or marriage breaks the linkage upon which many friendships are based.

People often use friendship as a balance against a lack of success in either the marital or occupational role. Being married, having children, and working creates a pool of emotional resources for people. If one or more of those roles lets a person down, the emotional pool can be topped off with friendship. The older person who gave friendship high priority before retirement generally does best after retirement.

Zena Blau in her book, *Old Age in a Changing Society*, wrote:

> Bonds of friendship, as a rule, develop only between people who view each other as equals and who have interests and experiences in common that they can freely share with one another. For these reasons, friendships are usually confined to people of the same generation and at a similar stage in life.[3]

I almost agree with Blau's statement. Remove the "same generation" requirement and emphasize stage—not age—matching, and I do agree. Implicit in the quote is a social custom that has outlived its usefulness.

Social scientists have shown repeatedly that middle-class men fulfill their intimacy needs primarily in marriage, while women find them in close relationships with other women. This is a consequence of the way we are socialized as children. After being taught to suppress feelings, young males rarely develop the skills to form intimate social friendships. The adult male's emotional independence generally makes close friendships less necessary and less possible.

The middle-class male's emotional limitations eventually drive his wife to friendships with other women. Widowed older men with high leverage in the marriage marketplace continue to seek friendship through marriage, and the low leverage of widows causes them to expand their group of intimate female friendships.

There are other ways of basing friendships. Friendships often serve as substitutes for major roles. The lack of a sense of satisfaction in marriage or work, even though successful, may create these compensating alternate emotional ties, but there is little understanding of their formation. My explorations suggest that restrictions on substitute friendships are much less stringent. The long-term bachelor, the spinster, or an only child are likely to be more flexible in forming friendships.

People who complement each other often seek mutual friendship. The pretty girl who wants company, and the unattractive girl who hopes for reflected attention, are seen in a restaurant. The brainy fellow with few social skills becomes a pal to the not-so-bright football player. In friends, as in lovers, we sometimes seek the qualities we don't possess.

How important is it that our friends be age-similar? Beth Hess, writing in *Aging and Society,* says:

> This normative emphasis becomes apparent as we realize the age similarity is seldom seen as a fact to be accounted for, whereas dissimilarity in age between friends may arouse suspicion, require explanation from the participants, or evoke societal control reactions ranging from ridicule to attempts to enforce separation. Age heterogeneity in friendship may be suspect because it appears to threaten deep-rooted assumptions about the very nature of the friendship bond: that people are held together by what they have in common.[4]

Hess goes on to say that society often views the basis of an age-different friendship as "pathological, immoral, or otherwise aberrant."

Hess has dramatically described the social stigma we have seen applied to other age-different relationships. Somehow her academic language makes the unions seem even more deviant.

Age-similar conditioning starts early. A traditional way of monitoring the development of children is to watch their interactions with friends. An older child who prefers to play with younger children is seen as "not wanting to grow up," or the reverse, "wanting to be the boss all the time." A young person who prefers older companions is suspected of being precocious, of trying to make up for some loss, of not learning what he's supposed to be learning, or of learning things he's not supposed to learn at his age. Some of these concerns reveal the insecurity of the adult supervisor. They also are a consequence of a basic axiom that permeates all of child raising and education: "Make the environment safe for the child."

And of course "safe," as far as society is concerned, means

developing the children along with their peer groups. It's far simpler from a mass education viewpoint, but it reinforces age-similar ties in unnatural ways. And worse, it blocks the richness of age-different friendships. A more liberal educator might say, "Let's make the child safe for the environment." Give the children an environment that is rich and diverse in experience, and let each child develop at his rate in his own direction under adult supervision.

Either society's fears or the practical matter of mass socialization of millions of children causes the formation of age-similar biases at an early age. The extent to which these early attitudes about age persist through adult life is not well understood. Some results suggest that the age factor becomes less important as we grow older and choose friends who are less like ourselves.

Adults get involved in actvities that cut across age lines, and that helps pull down the age barrier. As a middle-aged tennis player, I know men twenty years younger and older than I, who can defeat me in tennis any Saturday morning I may choose. However, as in childhood, age-different friendships may remain outside our culture's idea of normalcy whenever the friendships involve differences in social status, values, or life-styles.

It's interesting to speculate about the trade-off between proximity and similarity in making friends. Older people and children are often stuck in a group of others just like themselves, and the possibility of age-different friendships is slim. Studies of friendship in housing developments show that attachments are struck up between remarkably dissimilar people—if they live close together. The age-different walls constructed during youth crumble under these conditions. So often, however, neighborhoods are composed of fairly similar people.

In understanding the formation of friendships, I found it striking how, after decades of effort, researchers are finally recognizing the crudity of the age index as a measure of sharing in friendships. For example, people are quite ready to shift their loyalties to new friends if they no longer agree with old friends on certain issues. The age-similarity requirement dominant at the inception of a friendship falls away, and may not sustain the bond as the friend changes in other ways.

Old friends may not be best friends if sharing the passage of time and the progression of life stages means an unacceptable stage match at a later time. Friendships are not unlike any love relationship. Aside from other factors, their genesis depends on an initial sense of emotional opportunity—an attraction. Rarely is the beginning of a friendship thought of as a permanent connection. The inability of marriages to bear that burden of permanency is well documented.

The beginning of a friendship may be influenced by similarity and proximity, but its continuance depends on the perpetuation of something called "liking." The factors influencing the liking appear very complex, and are essentially a scientific enigma.

We can talk about the old adages "opposites attract," and "birds of a feather flock together." That's just a folksy way of saying friendships can be formed by people who are complements of each other or who are similar to each other. This observation immediately disregards age as a friendship criterion and places the emphasis on adult developmental stages. Stage, not age, determines the growth of an individual. Stage also characterizes a person's needs, and potential friends are attracted to each other because of similar and complementary sets of needs.

What a person gets or wants from a friendship may emerge clearly as time passes, but more likely it will be perceived very early by the partners. These perceptions will change as a friend's developmental stage changes.

If we both need the same things and are capable of providing them for each other, we are "birds of a feather." If each needs different things from the other and we can supply them, we are "opposites." I mentioned complementary friends earlier. Now both similar and complementary friends can be thought of in terms of stage, not age.

That, of course, is the major point. Chronological age is not a good indicator of developmental stage. There are many different indications of stage—maturity milestones, such as working full time, marriage, or parenthood.

People meeting each other have the ability (and it can be improved) to perceive an individual's development along physical, personal, and social lines. That growth implies a set of strengths and needs, and each person decides on that basis whether or not the friendship should proceed. During the lifetime of the friendship we, often without being aware of it, are reexamining the rationale for the existence of friendship. When the needs/gratification balance is out of kilter, the friendship may not be enriching and may be reduced in intensity or terminated.

As we introduce the participants in age-different friendships, watch for stage matching and the balance of needs/gratification.

Here is Kevin, thirty-five, telling of his friendship with Harry, sixty-six:

The circumstances of my meeting with Harry were rather complicated. You might be tempted to reject our friendship as just another job-related association, but it wasn't that way at all. I was in a very sticky spot in my life, and I met Harry just then.

At the time it felt like my career was going down the tubes. After five years of teaching engineering in a university, what I suspected all along became crystal clear. I would be unable to continue my teaching without completing my doctorate. In earlier years in the engineering profession, a master's degree was all it took, but times changed, and I was caught in the middle.

It seemed like I was too far in a career to back out, but completion of the degree was an impossible dream. After several years of evening, weekend, and summer work, I had painfully completed the necessary courses, but my wife and children were very unhappy about my constant distraction. I had no idea how to finance the year it would take to do a dissertation. More importantly, I wasn't dead sure I wanted to. The emotional scar tissue was getting rather thick on me.

I vacillated for a couple of years, then a new possibility opened for me. My alma mater offered a fellowship to finance the necessary year of work. I was happy, sad, and frightened all at once. It meant going fifteen hundred miles to the Midwest to do some work I wasn't sure I could do, to complete a degree I wasn't sure I wanted.

My family and I were in turmoil with the decision. Finally, I decided to go alone and make a major effort for a year to finish. My family would stay put and keep their fingers crossed. I tell you all this to give an idea of the mood I was in when I arrived at the university.

I rented a bedroom in the home of a widow, planned to eat

in the cafeteria, and plunged into my work. My life at that time is best described as "monastic." My research filled my days and nights, leaving room for nothing else.

At this point Harry came into my life. I had met him years earlier, but we never had any real contact. A senior professor, near retirement, he kept a very low profile in the department. I can't remember how our friendship began. I guess that one of our routine hellos turned into a coffee invitation. After that we met frequently for dinner, and eventually there were invitations for weekend trips.

At first I couldn't figure what Harry saw in me. Harry taught his courses, pursued many hobbies, and had that relaxed kind of relationship with his wife that only forty years can bring. He had a lot of casual university friends, but no real intimates.

In the beginning I was afraid to say no when he asked me to do something. I suppose I feared he might discredit me in some way with other faculty. I was also worried about taking time away from my studies. Both fears were unfounded. Harry didn't have a mean bone in his body, and without his diversion I probably would have gone crazy with day and night studies.

I grew to anticipate and enjoy my time with Harry. Because he knew exactly what my limitations were, he was never intrusive. The major focus of our relationship was Harry's hobbies. He shared with me the worlds of watch and clock collecting, rifle target shooting, pistol collecting, and eating. We've been known to drive two hours over back-country roads for a piece of special pie.

Harry set the ground rules for our friendship. It was all unspoken. He let me know indirectly what interested him and when he was available. Sometimes we would refuse invitations from each other, but that never made any difference. I never noticed his or my feelings being hurt. I loved being with him, and though he never said so, Harry enjoyed my company.

Harry controlled our conversations, too. Anything he didn't want to talk about, he just ignored. He talked on two levels— casually ninety-nine percent of the time, and intensely the other one percent. When one of his rare serious chats popped out, I caught a glimpse of the magnificent intellect of the man. I always felt incompetent and backed off.

I realize now that Harry was great at "making do." He sampled everything there was—where he was. He was never concerned, or even spoke, about wanting something else, somewhere else.

Like a puppy, I tagged along, just happy to be going. A midwestern winter taxes the ingenuity, but Harry always thought of things to do: a new restaurant, target shooting in his basement, an antique-clock collectors' meeting, or hiking across remote farm lands.

Harry didn't drink, but he seemed to like to watch me drink beer. I suspect he liked to see me loosen up a little. Often Harry's wife would join us on an outing, especially for eating, but he was the same no matter the circumstances.

Harry made a horrible year tolerable. One day he appeared at my office window. He motioned for me to unlock it, and when I did he threw it open and stepped in. As he came through the open window, a gust of wind hit my desk and sent the pages of an early draft of my thesis spinning around the room. Harry closed the window, lumbered to a chair, and watched me as I gathered pages from the floor and tried to reconstruct my thesis. As I fussed with the pages, Harry's only comment was, "I presumed you would write that thesis so that the pages read well in any order."

When my year at the university ended and I left with my doctorate in hand, my life with Harry ended as abruptly as it had begun. For a while we sent notes back and forth, but then he retired and I lost touch with him.

I'll never forget the man. Besides his time and warm interest for a year, Harry gave me an invaluable gift that I will cherish the rest of my life. Harry helped me stop being afraid of old people. Maybe "afraid" isn't the word, but all my life, before Harry, I felt blocked from making contact with elderly folks I didn't know. Something about them put me off and held me back. Harry was the first of a group of friends who are much older than I, and I am eternally grateful for having them in my life.

A form old-young friendships often take is that of confidant and confessor.[5] Between close age-different friends, the older person is often allowed access to relatively large portions of the younger person's private life. As Pamela explained:

My older friends are close because I've told them things about myself that I wouldn't tell just anyone—like personal things, about my private life, some problem I have or some detail about, say, my family life. It's not necessarily a problem, but something extremely private, like if my parents are probably getting a divorce, and I don't want many people to know about it. Sometimes Alexis [thirty-four years older] makes a casual comment that just clears my head. But, above all, I trust her completely.

The roles of confidant and confessor get mixed, as this comment from Alexis shows:

We have long talks about things. I confide in Pam, but with other people I'm limited in what I'll tell them about me. And our talks are pretty much open to any topic. We've told each other things that we don't tell other people—other than our husbands —and maybe a few things that we haven't told our husbands. Especially intimacies. There's no one else I would talk about that to. My husband knows basic things, but I don't go into detail with him, and I don't want him to go into detail with me [laugh]. So Pam and I can share details that wouldn't be right for anyone else's ears.

Pam revealed another crucial part of her friendship with Alexis when she talked about being able to be her uncensored self in their relationship.

I can share my most intimate feelings with her. Things like how I'm feeling about other people or where my life is going. There's no acting with her at all. I can be completely myself. I can approach that with some other friends, but with Alexis it's all the way.

Close friends often serve as substitute family members. Here is Kay, twenty-two, talking about Max, forty-three.

Our friendship is very much the relationship of a fond older brother and younger sister. He's an only child and so am I. Many years separate us, and yet we have many common interests and a great deal of affection for one another. It's the best part of a brother-sister relationship without any of the drawbacks. We both have someone to turn to if we want to, without having anyone making demands on you because of a family relationship.

Mutual attraction of some kind is almost always at the roots of friendship. This attraction translates into a desire for contact between friends, while each maintains a private life. Contact is a matter of choice, not pressure. Al, thirty-two, and Helen, fifty, are long-time friends. Al says:

I suppose that one indication of my attitude was when my wife and I got back from Europe. I think we got here and slept for maybe four or five hours at the most and then went over to Helen's. I never thought about it much at the time, but that shows where we headed when we got back. It just seemed natural. And I remember when I walked in the door. Helen was on the phone, and her husband, Fred, said, "Boy, is she going to be glad to see you." That made me feel so good.

Sam and John started their law practices at the same time. They have an eighteen-year age difference, but John began his law career late. They rented adjacent offices in the same building and met first as neighbors. This quote is from Sam.

John and I would sit in here and talk for three hours. No phones would ring, and no human being would walk down the hall. In the beginning we had plenty of time for the development of a friendship. We were so fortunate then, because that kind of time doesn't exist any more. John has developed a very busy tax practice, and I'm gone a lot on trial work. I think we are a good example of how a friendship can wither somewhat because of lack of time. I suspect that friendships go through stages, and John and I aren't as tight, or at least we don't have the occasions to confirm our tightness, as much as we did before. But I think the friendship endures in spite of the competition it faces. It's not something I worry about. I have a long-term faith in our friendship.

John and Sam are a classic example of changing needs in friendships. There is an ebb and flow of the amount of personal distance between them, but the basic connection is never threatened.

Mutual gratification of respective needs is an important aspect of a close friendship. The means by which the needs are met, however, are not simplistic. Among close friends there is a tendency to avoid translating mutual caring into complicated patterns of trading tangible favors and services. Close friends feel free to call on one another for help in times of need, but generally do not exercise that option to any degree. There is a great deal of emphasis on a friend perceiving the need, and then voluntarily offering to help.

Joan, twenty-one, and her office manager Karen, thirty-seven, have developed a close friendship outside the office. Joan had just moved into a new apartment when we talked to her about Karen.

I probably wouldn't have asked her to do most things, simply because the best part of doing things for a friend is when it is based on an offer. When you see that a friend needs something, or needs some kind of help, and you can do it or at least assist, then that's when you offer, rather than waiting until they actually ask for help. When I need someone to talk to or need help with this or that, just knowing that my dear friend is there and will recognize the need is wonderful.

Age-different friends are more likely to involve two people with different skills. Most of the age-different friends we interviewed were very conscious of not wanting to let their relationship become dominated by work or some kind of problem-oriented interaction. Too great an emphasis on favors or aid creates a sense of drudgery. Karen responded to Joan's remark above by saying:

I was going to paint my house, and Joan offered to come over. That was very nice, but she didn't have to do that. I don't like to intrude by asking a whole lot of favors. It never entered my mind to ask her. Frankly, I didn't want to do the painting either. It's a hard job and requires pretty good painting skills. Things that I would ask her to do would be things like giving me a ride home, or going down to pick up my car. Things she didn't really have to go out of her way a whole lot for. I believe that if you ask for too many favors all the time, you weaken the personal side of a friendship.

The most important basis for maintaining a close friendship is that a good feeling comes from most any kind of interaction, and that feeling lasts a long time. In other words, it isn't just the intimacy or the sense of community that close friends have, but the quality of interaction that occurs because of these characteristics. John, of John and Sam a few pages back, put it this way:

My conception of what constitutes a really good friendship is like this. I feel comfortable because I can be completely candid, and I feel enough sense of a stability so that any momentary dealings, whether good or bad, the relationship will endure in spite of those or because of those. You don't have to worry about it. You don't have to think about it. You don't have to do anything to cultivate it.

Age-different friendships that offer satisfying comfortable involvement are no different from others. They flourish on a foundation of shared interest, mutual understanding, and a sense of acceptance and trust. Age is not a requirement. Personal similarity, including chronological age, may contribute to the existence and stability of this foundation; however, true friendship is based on growth as people and the resulting expansion of the relationship. A core of similarity may support a budding friendship, but expansion of a sphere of commonality and the acceptance or toleration of one another's differences are essential for true richness in friendships.

Let's take a closer look at the impact of change on close friendships. This is particularly important in an age-different friendship, where the participants are likely to be changing at different rates.

The change with the most potential for impact on a friendship is a change in basic values and goals. These kinds of changes cause an overhaul of what a person finds interesting and important in life, and of how he sees and understands the world. Changes such as getting married, having a child, or moving to a new location generally do not alter values and life goals, and close friendship can endure.

Bob retired from the telephone company two years ago, and lives alone on a quiet suburban street. Cindy, twenty-five, lives two doors away with her daughter Lisa. Bob is widowed and Cindy is divorced. Since Bob retired and has been around the house, he and Cindy have become good friends—at least until recently.

In the last year I've become rather uncomfortable with Cindy. She spoils Lisa so, and I've become terribly uncomfortable when I'm around the two of them. I hate to criticize Cindy for the way she's raising Lisa, but I find myself doing it. And Cindy's a procrastinator. In the last year she's stopped working at her life. Now she just waits for problems to go away. I can't stand being critical, so I avoid her more and more.

Friendships have no visible contracts that give specific duties and responsibilities. Appropriate actions in a close friendship are generally based on perceptions. If there isn't enough closeness to allow good perceptions, or if there is a poor match of people and the perceptions are weak or erroneous, the friendship fails.

These perceptions work both ways, and the desired result is an exchange of rewards and services in close friendship. Generally, people expect a balance in the exchange. There is usually present a moral responsibility to repay in kind the rewards and favors granted by a friend. This is a very subtle factor. It flows naturally from mutual liking and caring, and is not tallied somewhere on a ledger. There is an intuitive link between an assurance of help and a history of good interactions. An acquaintance of mine, talking about one of his friends, said:

I'd do anything for him, and I felt he'd do anything for me. I guess it was just a gut feeling. Of course, what proof did I have that I could borrow a thousand dollars from him because I needed it? I never really tested it. We did things together and felt good together, and I just knew I could.

Many friends said that if there were too much attention paid to patterns of exchange, then the bond between the individuals would not be that strong.

Coeval friends, when they are very close, often describe their friendship as a kind of sanctuary. Together, two people create a special world in which they can relax and be themselves. It is this quality of sanctuary that coeval friends have the most difficulty imagining in age-different friendships. It is as though the sense of sanctuary is dependent upon a high degree of conventional similarity. Not so, as Joe will explain.

I first met Marge when I was still in college. I was taking five years to do a four-year bachelor's degree, and she was finishing her doctorate. At first I felt too dumb around her, and our twenty-one-year age difference was very strange for me. Marge ran one of my lab sections, and after the class was over we stayed in touch. There was some kind of special liking between us, and our friendship grew in importance. It turned out that we had the same basic ideas of how we should live and be, but we went about it in very different ways.

Marge was very direct, and had a strong sense of right and wrong. I would be much more influenced by others. Someone might want me to try this or that dope, and I would. I'd go as far as I could, and then when I was about to go off the deep end, I'd go see Marge. She was like a breath of fresh air for me. With her I could get into the good life again. You know—smell the flowers and see the sky. When I spent time with Marge I had a great time, and I didn't have a hangover the next morning.

It was as though I could lead a double life. With other friends I could go in any crazy direction I wanted to, then I'd go see Marge to get straightened out.

When we talked to Marge, she told us what she got from Joe in exchange for the sanctuary she offered him.

We tend to turn to each other when we need support, and my needs are very different from Joe's. Last year my widowed mother became incompetent, and I had to take care of everything for her. I felt absolutely rotten about putting her in a nursing home, even though I knew it was the right thing to do. Joe supported me in so many ways. He did dozens of errands connected with the medical and legal issues, and he has that unending faith in my standards. He never wavered for a moment in his support of my decision. I needed that.

Sometimes the secret world which friends create for each other is a place where no seriousness is allowed. There is no requirement for performance. This, too, is a special kind of sanctuary. My dear friend, Shirley, was like that with me. For a long time she was my teacher. She opened up a new world of metaphysics for me, but my scientific background collided with her beliefs in painful ways at times. When her emotion met my intellect, and there was an impasse, we went, without hesitation, to a special place.

Shirley became "Maud," and I was "Clyde"—just two old folks down on the farm. We'd talk for a while about the vegetable crops and the weather, and then I'd get on Maud about the way she blew the egg money every time she went to town.

I would turn to Shirley and say, "Dammit, Maud, I am so pissed at you," in a way I never could in the real world. Shirley and I would stay in our unsophisticated country world where everything was said straight out, until we blew off steam and could return. I suppose it was our private way of laughing at ourselves, and not having it hurt.

Emma and Janet met at church. They have been friends for about four years. Neither would admit her age, but Emma is a sixtyish widow, and Janet is divorced and in her early forties. They both have routine jobs. Emma works part time and lives alone not far from Janet; they would be described by most people as ordinary. Their close friendship has taken the form of reducing the humdrum in their lives.

QUESTION: How do you have fun together?

JANET: We do things together, like the grocery shopping. These activities are normally a pain, and we turn them into fun. We allow plenty of time, check all the bargains, share ideas on new things, and never worry about having to wait in line. People must think we're crazy sometimes. Here we are, standing at the end of a long line of people with huge baskets of food, and we are smiling, laughing, and chatting. Sometimes one of us will take a magazine off the stand and read the jokes to the other. Or we'll read and laugh at those ridiculous newspapers with the sensational stories.

EMMA: It's not just avoiding loneliness. We've found that when you're doing tedious jobs, it's nice to have someone around to share the tedium. Maybe you don't think that's much of a friendship, but Janet and I love our time together. She makes the disagreeable parts of my life so much more tolerable.

JANET: You should have seen us a couple of Sundays ago. Here we are, dressed in work clothes, up on the roof trying to assemble and mount my new TV antenna. After an hour of fumbling around, we just sat down on the roof and laughed and laughed at our mechanical stupidity. But you know, we're not really so dumb. We finally got that darn thing up, even though a shower drenched us just before we finished.

EMMA: We do other things, too. Sometimes we help each other escape or recover from a bad scene. Last month I had a whole bunch of relatives descend on me for a week. I thought I would go out of my mind. In the middle of the week, Janet called me in the evening and got me over here for a couple of hours. I was so grateful, but best of all was what she did on the day they left. She invited me for dinner and treated me like a queen. She served all my favorite dishes, and later she gave me a wonderful back rub. I got so relaxed I fell asleep. Almost didn't get home that night.

JANET: We give each other advice sometimes, too. Our lives are quite similar. Our home, our work, and our friends are the extent of it. But we both have family that make things complicated now and then. We've both been married, so we have our own families and in-laws, too.

EMMA: Remember the time your former mother-in-law came for a visit and tried to talk you into going back with your ex-husband? [*Janet nodding.*] Janet was a mess that day. She came over here and started talking about the whole business. I sat her down and asked what it was she wanted out of life. She started to say this and that—but I made her write it down. I got that old chalk board—used to belong to the kids—out of the basement, stood Janet up there and made her write everything down.

It soon became clear that there was no need in her life that any ex-husband was going to take care of.

JANET: Emma's right, except we don't really give each other advice. It's more like we help each other clarify things. Sometimes we do it even when it isn't asked for. I remember when Emma's youngest daughter came and stayed with her last year. She stayed and stayed and stayed, and finally I asked Emma what was going on. It turned out that she didn't even know. Enid had been there for a month, and she and Emma had not had a heart-to-heart talk. So they sat down and really talked to each other and worked things out.

EMMA: Sometimes when I see Janet about to do a silly thing, I'll ask her to think it over, or I'll offer to gather some more information before she makes up her mind. She was about to invest in a piece of property a while back, but I got a real estate friend to check it out, and he talked Janet out of it.

QUESTION: Aren't you afraid you'll damage your friendship by getting involved in personal and financial matters?

JANET: I never think about it.

EMMA: Me either. I just react. I suppose I trust Janet to know that I have good intentions.

In visiting with many age-different friends, it was very clear that one of the most valued attributes of the relationships was openness. Nearly everyone pointed out that it is possible to live a very long time on this globe without having someone open up and share from the top to the bottom of his being what it is like for him to be in the world. It is a rare relative who will be that revealing about the depths of his soul.

Rollo May, the famous psychologist, has said that human intimacy is based on an individual's willingness to reveal his dreams, fears, and fantasies to another. Dear friends tell me that they come closer to experiencing that kind of intimacy in friendships than in their marriages.

Here is a comment made by an interviewee about a friend.

She is a rather open and very deep human being, who is capable of talking about herself with a great deal of intelligence. I've watched her over a long period of time, and my admiration for her

insightfulness grows. She has made interesting observations
about other people. Once, after a meeting, she drew my attention to
the fact that a person made me more angry than even I realized.
I found that when I relived the situation in my mind, she was
absolutely right. She is always genuinely interested in what is
going on inside me, and I find that flattering. I want a friend
who has done some serious thinking about her own life—
what it means to her—and is willing to share that with me. That
is the most valuable quality I seek in a friend.

Listen to Ben talk about Andrew:

I'm interested in what he has to say. I don't agree with all his
opinions, but I want to hear them. He is like a window for me.
He's in his middle thirties, and I'm going into my middle fifties,
and Andrew provides a special view of the generation behind
me. You know, that's a full generation! He is an active member
of a generation that is now moving into my world of the
bureaucracy of the state. Our friendship has developed around his
willingness to be completely open about his thinking and attitudes,
and my interest in them.

Ben went on to say:

Our friendship and interaction goes something like this. Recently
we went to a meeting at the state capitol. We saw that meeting
and listened to it with eyes and ears twenty years different in age.
You take those two reactions and mix them in a close friendship,
and special things happen. We trade ideas, observations, and
insights back and forth, and the sparks fly. When that discussion
is over we have grown a little, and we know more about what
went on at that meeting than we dreamed of before. As we talk,
I realize how excited I am about what I have going on with
Andy. It's so special I can't really articulate the uniqueness of it.
Never, in the past, have I had a friendship like this. I figured
the young guys couldn't tell me anything I didn't know, and I
have to admit that I didn't think he would be interested in me
anyway—except to exploit me in some way. I've had plenty of
contacts like that with young fellows. You know—we get together

because we need something from one another. Then after we each get what we want, we're back to talking about baseball and the weather.

We asked what was different about Andrew.

BEN: I instinctively liked him. In our very first conversation we talked as peers. I had no sense of age difference. In fact, we seemed so much alike in the way we approached things. He never talked up or down to me. There were things he wanted and he said so, but I never felt exploited.

QUESTION: Are there any limits on your friendship?

BEN: Yes and no. There are parts of our life that are not well connected, but that's more like circumstances than choice. We rarely get together with our wives in the evening, but we live so far apart. We met through the bureau, and so many of our meetings are bureau related. And of course I travel a lot. We don't have the same circle of friends, so there are lots of obvious limitations. But amongst all these barriers we've carved out a niche for ourselves, and friendship thrives there. We've had to be very specific. We meet for lunch at least once a week, dinner every month, and we take some sort of a weekend trip together every six months. This structure evolved, and it's kind of our way of showing our friendship its proper priority. We have occasional business meetings and plenty of telephone calls, but our informal schedule is the foundation of everything. It's been over four years now, and as I think about it, we have developed a kind of pattern together. We went through a period of exploring common interests and all that sort of thing. We found that just meeting to talk wasn't enough for us. We wanted some activity that we could do together. It turned out to be fly fishing—believe it or not. You know, it's a wonderful art, and it turned out we both had been thinking about getting into it. So we have this new parallel, ongoing activity which gives us something else. We're both so damned verbal. Our weekend trips are almost always to some special stream. I've even become involved in tying my own flies, but Andy just laughs and says the store-bought kind is just as good. So we have this little ongoing competition.

QUESTION: Are there any limitations on what you discuss?

BEN: Not consciously. We've never started a conversation and had to back off. We have become very sensitive to each other, and each is available for unlimited listening. We don't talk about our skills in bed—that sort of thing. We seem to talk more about fears and anger than we do about love. Don't know why. You've made me consider just what it is that I like about my friendship with Andy. In two words—it's attention and caring. I know that I'm important to Andy, and that he's willing to give me some of his life energy. And most importantly, he's happy to have me reciprocate.

QUESTION: Do you ever have fights?

BEN: We can get rather testy at times. We've never fought, but we disagree, get angry, and then resolve it quickly. It usually has to do with bureau business, and it's always something political. I think that we are both very sensitive to the limitations of our friendship. Not that we aren't willing to test those limits constantly. If we sense that we're being resistant or evasive, we catch the cues very quickly, and one of us will back off. After that there may be a few quiet moments, and then we get on to something else. Neither one of us is interested in getting the other extremely uptight or angry. We both seem to know when that point is being approached.

QUESTION: In what ways do you affect one another?

BEN: Well, let's see—I've never really thought about this. Andrew probably keeps me looser and more youthful, and I suspect that my slightly more conservative viewpoint stabilizes him. I guess we see each other as models to some extent.

Close age-different friendships are indistinguishable from close coeval friendships. In both cases there is an initial mutual attraction, followed by the identification and satisfaction of a set of matching or complementary needs. An intimate relationship of this sort guarantees a maximum of individual integrity and freedom. These close age-different friendships have a family-like character—which gives a sense of community and belonging—yet still have the flexibility of friendship.

While the intensity may be lacking at times, this is compensated for by the possibility of tailoring the relationship to personal needs and desires. In this way a great deal of conflict is avoided. There is great emphasis on mutually enjoyable activities.

Age-different friendships are held together by a mutual desire to maintain the arrangement. A change in basic values, goals, and attitudes may cause the relationship to end.

Age-different friendships may be thought of as the middle ground between formalized personal relations and total individual autonomy. These friendships are a unique blend of maximizing pleasure and minimizing pain. Their potential for enriching one's life is high, because they meet personal needs and desires and allow for personal autonomy and self-directedness.

CHAPTER NINE

Those Who Didn't Make It

NOT EVERYONE IS successful in age-different relationships. Departure, disillusionment, divorce, or death will leave survivors who suffer and regret their age-different ventures. The younger member may feel his/her best years were wasted in an interaction that was all too brief. The older survivor often experiences depression, cynicism, and withdrawal, from the feeling of being alone during critical years. Others are merely sad that the potential personal enrichment was terminated.

Was the age barrier the problem? Were stages not properly matched? Were personal idiosyncracies present that were capable of blocking any relationship? Every problem that we explore will offer answers. We can learn from those who didn't make it. Let's take a look.

Can the classic May-December pattern of romance be reversed

to the woman-older/man-younger union? That is the first question. The answer is being decided in the media. During the two and one-half years we were interviewing age-different couples for this book, we found many more newspaper and magazine articles touting the woman-older couple than we found people living the life. We also found books, cartoons, comic strips, movies, and television shows using the theme, and most were promoting the woman-older/man-younger relationship. With the media's insatiable thirst for newness, especially if overtones of sensationalism are present, the man-younger couple gets plenty of press, and only secondarily is it positive press.

I sense that we are in a period of reaction to a new social alternative, not unlike the response to the man-older couple several decades ago. You know—the famous people have been doing it; now the ordinary folks are trying it. Some middle-class people are trying woman-older/man-younger unions, but the age differences are not large, marriage is rarely involved, the duration of the alliance is frequently short, and it is often unstable. The social stigma to be overcome by the woman-older/man-younger couple is still substantial, and most participants are subject to significant self-doubt. Because the media are filled with success stories, let's begin with a visit to a couple who exude the uncertainties we often found in man-younger age-different partnerships.

Jesalee and I met Ted and Pat in a small, modestly furnished apartment in a building on the outskirts of town. Ted, dressed very simply in sports shirt and slacks, is a slender, rather unattractive man with dark hair and olive skin. His demeanor whispers passivity. He has poor posture, with shoulders rounded and chest caved in. Standing or sitting, he slumps, and his voice is a monotone, while his eyes are always somewhere else.

Pat is as garish as Ted is colorless. She has short, bleached-blonde hair. She wears layered makeup, and a tight T-shirt emphasizing high, thrusting breasts. She has a good figure and smiles constantly, and her jewelry clatters as she moves around the room.

While we were there, Pat and Ted exchanged glances constantly—hers loving, his hopeless.

Ted had little to say about his childhood except that it was "normal." His father died when he was fifteen, and now, although his mother lives less than a mile away, he rarely sees her. His sister lives several states away, and they exchange Christmas cards.

In succession, Ted went through high school, the service, college, and a five-year marriage. He followed a middle-class path right to a divorce. He does fairly well as an accountant, but summarizes his marriage experience by saying, "I could never communicate with my wife."

I asked what that meant in practical living terms, and he answered, "We never argued, but each of us would go through wild emotional gyrations and never reveal them to the other. Ultimately, it was as though we were strangers to each other."

At age thirty, as he was divorcing his wife, Ted met Pat.

Pat's background was as exotic as Ted's was commonplace. Her father was a career foreign service officer, and she was raised in a variety of cultural settings—mostly South America. She is an only child, and although her father was harsh and domineering, she said, "He absolutely adored me." Her parents battled constantly, and the peace that followed her mother's death when Pat was seventeen was a blessing. She was sent to boarding school and hated it. A series of stepmothers passed in parade—"all neurotic." In spite of all this Pat insisted that "All I've ever wanted to be is a good wife and mother."

At twenty-one, Pat married a twenty-six-year-old dentist and tried to pursue her dream. Success was incredibly elusive. First, there was a painful and frustrating four-year period when her husband trained for a specialty. Pat supported him by doing clerical work and "hating every moment of it." The first year was particularly difficult, and Pat admits to feeling suicidal during that time.

Even after her husband's practice began, he resisted beginning a family. Pat "poked holes in her diaphragm," but nothing happened. Eventually he agreed to try to have a baby, but still nothing happened. Finally they submitted to tests, and learned that they couldn't have a child together (she wouldn't say why).

They decided to adopt, and at thirty-three, Pat's dream of becoming a mother finally came true. Happily, her husband enjoyed being a father, but their marriage was subsequently damaged beyond repair by the problems of parenthood. They went from a double bed to twin beds, then to separate rooms on the same floor, separate rooms on different floors, and, finally, her husband had his own apartment on the third floor of their home, while Pat and their daughter lived on the first floor. He became cynical and abusive, and their ten-year marriage ended.

Pat's story became incoherent at this point. She rambled on about his involvement with work, her concern about security for her daughter, her pleading with him to have surgery on his nose to reduce the loudness of his snoring, and their incessant fighting. It was the jumbled chronicle of an overstressed marriage that became bizarre and vengeful at the end.

It seems clear that both Pat and her ex-husband were left emotionally damaged in the aftermath of their shattered marriage. He fled the state, and two years later Pat married a man nine years younger than she. The marriage lasted less than a year. "He would never talk to me," she said.

For the next fifteen years, Pat held a series of mediocre jobs and tried to raise an increasingly rebellious daughter. "She's been running away since she was nine." During that period, Pat was engaged three times to men near her age. She described herself as "super selective," and is delighted that none of those affairs worked out.

When she was forty-eight, she met Ted, twenty-eight, and they have been going together for two years. There have been several breakups during that time. Four months ago, they married. Recently they began living apart again, and Ted returned to Pat's apartment for our interview.

QUESTION: Where are you living now, Ted?

TED: I have my own apartment.

PAT: Isn't that crazy! That's the same apartment he had when I met him two years ago. He's never let it go. Not even after we were married. [*Ted remains expressionless and says nothing.*]

QUESTION: How did you meet?

PAT: For many years I've been involved with singles clubs. I was hostessing a singles bridge party right here in my apartment, and Ted came. He started asking me out right away, but all we ever did was go to more bridge parties. It was so silly, because he's a thousand times better player than I am.

TED [*interjecting*]: We went to two.

QUESTION: Was either of you aware of your age difference when you started going out?

PAT: I never even thought about it.

TED: I admit it bothered me for a while. My mother commented about it in a way that made me uncomfortable. But the worst part was my friends. Most of my friends are younger than I am, and Pat's friends are older. We soon found out that they didn't mix well. I think I'm more comfortable with it now.

QUESTION: Why did you get married?

TED: Because I was miserable being apart from her. We lived together for about six months—I moved out—then we maintained kind of a funny relationship back and forth.

PAT: I wanted to get married because I'm old-fashioned. Never in my whole life have I changed about what I want to do. I want to be domestic. I want to be a housewife. I want to be married. Another part is practical. When we were living together I was giving my all, and I wanted some of the fringe benefits that a wife receives. Like health insurance—I have no protection if I get really sick.

QUESTION: You had a recent breakup. What is the problem?

PAT: Oh, God. I just went to a marriage counselor today. Ted goes tomorrow. [*A long silence follows. Neither one seems willing to begin.*]

PAT: [*blurting out*]: Trust. That's our problem.

TED: [*interrupting*]: It's more like communication.

QUESTION: What is the trust issue?

PAT [*giggling very nervously*]: Now don't kill me, dear, but once when we had a little tiff, Ted left, spent the night with an old girlfriend, and lied about it the next day.

QUESTION: Do you have an agreement for a monogamous relationship?

TED: That's acceptable.

PAT: Yes, as long as he's monogamous. I'm as attracted to the opposite sex as he is, and the first moment he wavers from our agreement—I'm gone.

QUESTION: Do you see any disadvantages to being married to a younger man?

PAT: Oh, no. I see all the advantages. Sex, for one thing.

QUESTION: Better sex than with a man your age?

PAT: Of course. They're all impotent. I've found many men are impotent in their forties. It's very, very sad.

QUESTION: Other advantages?

PAT: I'm a goer, and interested in many things, and I think a younger man is more adaptable, vital, and has the energy to stay up with me.

QUESTION: Is it your experience that men in their sixties have low energy?

PAT: I've oversold my point. Two of my dearest friends, platonic relationships, are in their sixties, and they are ready to go any time.

TED [*interrupting*]: You see. She can have platonic friends who are older, but when I choose younger platonic friends, that's a no-no.

PAT [*a bit miffed*]: If I had younger platonic friends, you wouldn't like that either.

QUESTION: Is your relationship open to the possibility of each of you having nonsexual friends of any age?

TED: Not if it's one-sided.

PAT: Ted knows all my friends, but I know hardly any of his. The unknown frightens me.

QUESTION: Is either of you jealous of the other?

TED: Pat's very jealous.

PAT: If I weren't jealous of Ted, it would be the same as saying I don't care about him. If I wholeheartedly throw myself off the cliff about somebody, I always am jealous.

QUESTION: Let's get back to advantages. Ted, what advantages do you experience in being married to an older woman?

TED: In the beginning, I didn't think there were many, because of the social pressure—

PAT [*breaking in*]: What social pressure?

QUESTION: Did people stare when you went out in public?

TED: No, Pat's personality and appearance are so youthful, that never happens. I think that as far as our personality levels and everything else go, we're at the same age.

QUESTION: What is your forecast for your future?

PAT: I'm optimistic. It's the same old dull story. I want to be a happily married wife and homemaker. I expect to have a better relationship with my daughter. I expect to be an asset to Ted, and he to me.

TED: I'm optimistic too, though I confess I worry from time to time because of pressures.

PAT: What pressures?

TED: A good example of being pressured is the way I felt when I saw the prices of houses we looked at. My monthly payments would be astronomical.

PAT: I assume you are expecting to get future salary increases.

TED: Houses have been going up a lot faster than my salary. Pat wants the domestic scene, but a house will block many of the fun things we do together. We still relate to the style of the singles scene—trips, vacations, and fancy restaurants.

PAT [*bitterly*]: This is so strange. After all, we're jet setters. You know, we maintain two residences.

TED: It's been tough at times. I moved out five days after we were married, but we are well along on a serious reconciliation attempt now. We love each other very much.

QUESTION: Why did you respond to our ad and agree to be interviewed when your relationship appears to be in a tender condition?

PAT: I didn't think about our problems at all. Your study is fascinating to me, and I wanted to meet you. And I'm confident we are going to make it over all the pitfalls.

TED: We've gone through a lot.

PAT: I think all of this has drawn us closer together.

TED: We're learning slowly, but we're learning. We'll always be together.

PAT: Ted has this steadfast devotion to me. It's super neat.

QUESTION: Ted, were you nervous about discussing your relationship with us?

TED: No, not really. I've already reviewed a lot of this with my therapist.

QUESTION: Do you have any suggestions for people who are considering age-different relationships?

PAT: I want us to be a super neat example for other people. It can be done. Age is a lot of baloney. Love, respect, and caring are what counts. It will be like completing a mission in life if I can be a good example to others. I want to support the old-fashioned idea of marriage and commitment. In the last two years our friends have seen us go through so many stages, and I want to show them we can make it.

TED: It's very important for you to remember that our problems have nothing to do with age difference. We have been accepted socially, and that's the biggest hurdle.

We have followed the reconciliation attempt of Pat and Ted for some time. They still live separately. Pat told me during a telephone call recently that she realizes she's trying to remake the world to fit a girlish dream, but "that's the way I am." Our impression of Ted is that inwardly he wants to be free and independent, but his fears cause him to seek a very different outside world. The result is confusion and uncertainty.

The outcome for the previous couple is still uncertain, but there's no uncertainty about our next age-different couple. They have been divorced for five years, after having been married for less than two. They met when Bill was forty-three and Ann twenty-four. They were lovers for a year and a half, lived together for a brief period, and then married and had a child. Both are happily remarried now, and we interviewed them separately. Here is Ann, beginning the story of an unsuccessful age-different marriage we will examine from two different viewpoints.

I'm basically a country girl, straight off the Great Plains of Kansas. Family means everything to me, but forming a successful family of my own eluded me for years. Can't say I didn't try, though.

I began by marrying my high school sweetheart the hard way. He had already gone to college in Chicago when I had to call him with the news I was pregnant. He was unhappy about that, but the families got together, and the next thing I knew I was married and living in Chicago.

Big deal. I got to support Bob all through his law degree. I had no skills and could qualify for only crappy jobs, but eventually I learned secretarial skills and did office work after that.

Those years were so difficult for me. Our marriage was okay, but Bob was constantly working on his studies. My boy, Stan, was born six months after I settled in Chicago, and Sue came along in three years. Later, I had another girl who died three weeks after birth. I've never gotten over losing her. It's been years ago, but I still cry about her.

Bob never wanted to be a college student with a family. He

couldn't do anything about Stan, of course, but the only way I could get pregnant after that was to have "accidents." Bob's idea of a good evening was to go out drinking with his buddies.

I worked as much as I could, but we still had to depend on our folks for some help. My kids were practically raised by baby-sitters. But somehow I was making it all happen. I had my family, and the employment future for my husband was bright.

That last year, when we were so near our goal, everything went sour. I suppose more than six years of struggle since high school had taken its toll. Years of living in a trailer, dressing my kids in hand-me-downs, constructing every kind of casserole known to mankind, and never having enough fun got to both of us.

I was starting to anticipate stopping work when Bob began to come up with his wild schemes. Every day it was something new—leave Stan and Sue at my folks' and hitchhike to South America; catch a freighter to Europe; join the Peace Corps; or go to San Francisco and join the hippies. By this time Bob had long hair and a beard.

I didn't know what to do. Every time I asked for details, Bob didn't have any. I told him he was acting more like he was about to graduate from high school than from law school. We started fighting a lot.

At some point near Bob's graduation, a switch inside me turned off. I decided Bob was not in my future, and I raised my head and started looking at the world around me.

Then, like magic, Bill came into my life. He was a senior manager in the company where I was working, and he had just been transferred to our branch. We instantly liked each other, and I could tell he enjoyed it any time I did some typing for him.

Bill had been divorced a few years earlier, and he seemed to be everything Bob was not. He was stable, confident, highly respected professionally, and full of fun. I knew he was older, but I never thought about it.

By now Bob and I were separated. Bill was making no personal moves towards me, so I decided to take the bull by the horns. One night at a company dinner, I was sitting next to Bill. We drank wine and chatted in a casual way. I turned to him and said,

"I just want you to know that if you ever want a woman, I'm available."

I could tell he was startled and pleased. We became lovers that night. Our courtship lasted a year and a half, and we went through many ups and downs. We broke up many times, but always came back together.

Our main connection was sex. He was after me all the time. When he first started seeing me his life was complicated. He spent time with his children, had many single friends, and was into a lot of stuff I didn't know anything about. For a long while he insisted on being very secretive about our relationship.

I wanted more and more of his time and energy, and slowly I got it. By then my divorce from Bob was final, and I told Bill I wanted to get married. He was very negative, but eventually I persuaded him to move in with me, and one morning at breakfast I talked him into going to a justice of the peace. That night we were back home as man and wife.

Our marriage was short, but not simple. We seemed to have different attitudes on everything, and we argued a lot. A couple of months after we were married, I told him I wanted to have his child. I thought he would faint. I persisted, though, and after a while he gave in. I got pregnant immediately.

I love being pregnant. My body literally sings with the experience, but Bill wasn't there to hear it. As our life changed with my pregnancy, he seemed to fade away. When he wasn't working, he was buried in a book or taking a walk. He spent hours wandering through the streets of our part of town, and he rarely had much to say. Our sex stopped.

Julie was born prematurely. She was so tiny and sickly that she remained in the hospital for a month. It was such a hard time for all of us. It depressed me to look through a window and watch her struggle for each breath. When she finally came home my life with my three children began, but my life with Bill seemed over.

I finally had what I'd wanted all my life—a successful husband, a home, my children, and most of all, time. Now I had a chance to truly work and develop my children, and I was excited about redoing our house to make room for Julie.

Eleven months after Julie was born, and less than two years after we married, Bill moved out.

There was no big explosion. I had started revealing my disappointments to Bill. The truth of our life always angered him, and he would stalk away. After such a scene he told me he had decided to look for a place of his own. I didn't protest much. We were very quiet for a couple of days, and then he left.

That was years ago, and looking back, I have no regrets about our divorce. We both seemed to want different things from each other. All the strength I sensed in Bill wasn't available to me, and the excitement I had with Bill early in our courtship faded, and we could never recapture it again.

I suspect we were both lonely and lost when we met, and once those matters were taken care of, there was nothing else between us.

After interviewing Ann, it was months before we could get together with Bill. He worked for the same large company, but now lived several states away. He's over fifty now, and remarried in another age-different relationship. He was not entirely happy about our request to review his marriage to Ann, but he agreed. He did not know what Ann had told us. Here is the story of Ann and Bill in Bill's words.

When I was thirty-nine years old and had achieved everything I'd ever wanted, my life fell apart. I'd traveled all around the world as a single man, had a powerful college education, married an incredible woman, raised a family, and did well in my work. I wasn't rich, but I never thought of that as a goal.

So here I was, forty, at my personal pinnacle in every way, and I threw it all away. It was as though I had a bottled-up crazy part, and it broke out, forced its way to the surface, and changed my life.

I wanted excitement and change—and apparently at any cost. I got involved in all the stuff that was happening in the mid-sixties. I stopped getting haircuts and grew a beard. I fooled around with dope. I had an affair. I participated in picketing and peace marches. And of course I divorced.

A part of my manhood was released for the first time in my life. I felt like a hunter in the woods, completely free and living by my wits. What I really was, I suppose, was just another middle-class clod going through an identity crisis. And a part of me was very afraid.

Sometimes I felt like a deviant and malcontent, and didn't know what to do next. Eventually I went to see a psychiatrist. I thought I might be going crazy. Actually, he wasn't much direct help, but I picked up some clues.

I realized that whole parts of me were missing, or at least I was hiding them. The emotional, playful, compassionate, spiritual side of Bill had been layered over by a kind of crust of rationality that didn't let much through.

I settled down a bit, and over the next three or four years I spent some time looking for my "missing pieces." I read a lot, talked to other people having similar experiences, and eventually saw a therapist once a week for about a year.

What was the outcome? Nothing very startling. I felt a little wiser and I certainly liked and accepted myself a lot more. But my life went on, superficially at least, about the same. My alimony and child-support payments kept me in a tiny apartment, and I spent a lot of time alone. A parade of women passed through my life, but no one stuck.

And then I met Ann. I've thought and thought, and tried to figure out what it was that was special about Ann. She had a bright, open, smiling demeanor that was appealing to me. I immediately felt friendship towards her, and working with her was a pleasure.

She flirted with me a little, and that gave my battered ego a boost. I never, at least in the beginning, considered an emotional involvement with her, because she was too young, and we worked in the same place.

Everything changed the evening she bluntly offered herself to me. I was overwhelmed, and my penis jumped to attention. I was enormously flattered that a beautiful young woman would simply offer me sex. Any limitations I felt towards her fell away under a surge of sexual energy.

The sex was wonderful, and I could never get enough, but in most other ways we were instantly in trouble. I was a little wiser, but still a "wounded bird." I found myself wanting a secret affair with Ann, but she was on the track of something much more serious, and I felt pressures.

I understood that she was alone with two little kids, but I didn't want to step into that blank spot in her family. I was trying to take care of my own children. I was constantly uptight about our age difference any time we were in public. And I seemed to have a fair load of guilt about her. I'm part of a generation that is never comfortable about a sexual partner who doesn't have at least a remote possibility of becoming a marriage partner, and I didn't see her that way.

Ann remained solid about wanting the strongest possible tie to me, while I did an in-and-out thing. When my worries about her were too much for me, I'd pull back, then when I was lonely and horny, I'd return. I was trapped in a pattern I didn't have the strength to break.

Ann's reaction to my oscillations can be summarized in one word—manipulation. Our breakups brought wilder and more bizarre reactions from her. First, I would find gifts or notes in unexpected places, or at four in the morning she would come to my apartment and crawl naked into my bed. Later there was a suicide attempt, and sometimes she slept with other men to make me jealous. Everything worked. I always came back. Tears, a call about a sick child, or any contrived emergency, and I was there.

Recalling all this is strange for me. It's like remembering a bad dream. I still can't believe it really happened. Even back then, I knew intellectually what was going on, but I was helpless. There was something I needed from her at that time in my life, and that hook kept me attached to her.

Finally I made a major effort to escape. I took an out-of-town assignment for several months, and all I did was seal my doom. I was miserable without her. I wrote, telephoned, and arranged visits. At the same time, a different part of me tried desperately to connect with another woman. I found women, dated and slept with them, but one of us always discredited the other in some way. Nothing lasted.

When I returned from the trip, Ann convinced me to stay with her while I looked for a new apartment. We'd been seeing each other for a year and a half at that point, and I had made my peace with our age difference. Age was no longer a factor. In some ways I perceived Ann as older and wiser than I was.

In Ann's house, the pressure was on me. Nearly every day the

subject of marriage came up, and in spite of this I lingered.
I can remember exactly what happened to seal my fate. Earlier
during the sessions with the therapist, he had hammered on my
penchant for secrecy and caution. He had told me that these
qualities limited the richness of my life in insidious ways.

First, I tried openness. I searched my guts and told Ann
every fear and fantasy I had. I spilled it all, and nothing made
any difference to her. Next, I approached myself on the question
of risk. Again and again, I asked myself why I was resisting the
love of a beautiful young woman who wanted only to be
with me. I kept wondering whether my caution was the flaw in
our union, and if I were being my own worst enemy.

I literally talked myself into accepting the marriage overtures
of Ann. It was as though a little voice in my head kept
repeating, "Risk, you fool. Risk, and everything will be all right."
One morning I agreed with that voice, and by that evening Ann
and I were married.

As long as I live, I will never forget the evening of the day Ann
and I were married. As we talked quietly after that hectic day,
I became aware of subtle changes. The bittersweet trials and
tribulations of romance had been replaced by the reality of specific
responsibilities. Three more people now depended on me. At a
time when all I wanted was to be held and comforted, Ann
directed the pillow talk to buying a house, stopping work, and
tightening the family unit. We had a new pattern in our life,
and I couldn't oscillate anymore.

The die was cast and never faltered. I was a naive kid looking
for romance, and Ann was a matriarch intent on building her
family unit. I got what I wanted if she got what she wanted.

The most intimidating example of what I'm saying occurred
soon after we were married. Ann announced that she wanted
to have a child with me. I was shocked. I assumed that she always
knew I was "out of production." I had two, she had two—that
was sufficient. I was already having enough trouble getting
along with Stan and Sue. It was not easy for them to accept me.
Their loyalty was to Bob.

In every way I could, I tried to convince Ann that we should
not have a child, but she was immovable. The pressure mounted,
and finally she as much as said that without our own baby

we were through. I was genuinely trying to make our marriage work, and once again I gave in.

Ann was instantly pregnant, and then everything went wrong. She became even more maternal, and our sex life faded. The house I had purchased had to have a nursery, and the expenses were astronomical. Julie was premature and stayed in the hospital for more than a month. The medical bills were staggering.

Julie's painful beginning was hard on the entire family. Ann worried so much that she finally lost heart and became essentially nonfunctional. I was overworked, and Stan and Sue were always upset. Ann stopped going to the hospital, but I went every day to watch Julie fight for life.

Julie made it, but it wasn't easy. And even when she was okay, a new baby is hard on a household. I suspect now that any chance for our marriage to survive was blasted by these events. A week after Julie was born, I was sterilized to end that issue forever.

The rest of our time together was all downhill. I turned to my work for solace, and Ann focused on the kids. Our parting was anticlimactic. Ann was rather stoic about it. It finally became clear, even to her, how wrong the life we had constructed was for me.

I was demolished. Once again, I had failed in the same pattern as before. I had broken some barriers and was much more willing to risk, but not wise enough to avoid repeating my mistakes.

I've grown a lot since then. My emotional needs are more manageable, and my inner resources have multiplied manyfold. Thank goodness, I'm finally mellowing out a little.

There you have it—the two sides of an ill-conceived age-different romance. Both Ann and Bill are in stable positions in their lives now. When they were well clear of their previous marriages and could perceive their short- and long-term needs, each chose a more suitable mate.

In two and one-half years of interviewing age-different couples, the most common problem cited was the fear of early widowhood. Again and again, we were told that the average fifty-year-old woman has little leverage in the marriage marketplace. A small percentage of widows will seek younger men, but most want a coeval partner —with marriage or not.

Most widows emphasized that if they had their lives to live over, they would choose their age-different marriages again. Nevertheless, the prospect of up to twenty-five years alone at an advanced age frightened many.

We want you to meet Harriet, who at fifty-eight has been grappling with her widowhood for four years. When she was fifty-four, her seventy-four-year-old husband died, after twenty-seven years of marriage. Harriet "would not give up one moment of my marriage," and still wears her wedding rings. In the saga of her age-different union, we found the threads common to so many other widows' stories.

Harriet has been a nurse, working in San Francisco, for over thirty-five years. She epitomizes all that you might expect of someone in that humanitarian profession. A small, attractive woman, she carries simultaneously an aura of competence and of caring. She is quiet and retiring, but only a small interaction is necessary to betray the personal energy bubbling just beneath the surface.

QUESTION: How did you meet your husband, Joe?

HARRIET: I was working for a surgeon in San Francisco shortly after the end of World War Two. He and Joe were best friends, and through the doctor, I met Joe.

QUESTION: What was Joe like?

HARRIET: He was an incredibly romantic figure of a man. I was twenty-seven then, and he was forty-seven. He had been a ship's master for many years—mostly freighters. He sailed everywhere and had a million stories to tell. A year or two before I met him, he had become a harbor pilot in San Francisco Bay. He went out on a small boat to meet ships a few miles at sea. He was put aboard, and then he guided the ships through the fog and the treacherous currents of the Golden Gate, through the heavy ship traffic of the bay, and finally to their mooring places. It was an assignment reserved only for the most senior and competent captains.

He always wore his uniform with the gold braid turning green. A tall man, six foot six, he was a dashing figure. When the doctor introduced us, he gave me a hug and a kiss like he had known me forever. I fell in love instantly, and a year later we were married.

QUESTION: During that year, did you have any reservations about your age difference?

HARRIET: Yes. I knew I would live many years longer than Joe, and I wondered how I would face those years.

QUESTION: Did you ever think about an in-between time when Joe might be slowed down or even a semi-invalid, and you were still hale and hearty?

HARRIET: Not then. He was so alive and active those early years, but I thought about it later.

QUESTION: What did Joe think of your age difference?

HARRIET: He kidded a little, but it was rarely discussed. We never used our age difference as a weapon. He never said, "you're too young to understand." He never made me feel like I was incompetent, and I never said Joe was too old for this or that. We never hurt each other with our age difference.

QUESTION: Did you ever tell Joe you feared being a young widow?

HARRIET: I insisted that he give me very explicit burial arrangements. I suppose that betrayed a fear.

QUESTION: Were your family and friends opposed to your courtship with Joe?

HARRIET: My family was shocked and negative until they met him. Before we were married, we went to see everyone, and they all loved Joe. He was always friendly, outgoing, and unconcerned about our age difference, and that reassured them. Sometimes I felt like my friends and family liked Joe better than me.

QUESTION: What were the early years of your marriage to Joe like?

HARRIET: Wonderful. Joe and I had so much together, but I continued to have friends my own age. It's curious. I was never interested in another older man. The men who caught my attention along the street were almost always near my own age. We each had our own circle of friends our age, and they usually didn't know each other.

QUESTION: Was either of you ever jealous?

HARRIET: Never. And that's what made our marriage work. Each of us knew that what made us attractive to each other would make us attractive to other people. That was just accepted. If

I met a man for dinner, or Joe took a woman to lunch, nothing was thought of it.

QUESTION: When did you first notice Joe's energy starting to drop, while yours was still high?

HARRIET: I remember the turning point clearly. It was when Joe was nearly sixty-two, just before he retired. He sensed that his pilots' group no longer needed him the way they had, and he was being eased out. He had less responsibility then, and younger men were waiting to take his place. It hurt his feelings terribly. He came down with a very bad case of the retirement blues. It was all very abrupt. All of a sudden, I realized that our sex life together was over. I was devastated, but I decided not to push Joe. His health had started deteriorating, too. He learned he had sugar diabetes, and his energy just wasn't there. Joe was simply exhausted, physically and emotionally, after a long and busy life.

QUESTION: So there you are. You've had fifteen great years of marriage. You're forty-two, in the prime of your life, and your husband has become impotent. How did you handle that?

HARRIET: It was hard on me. At that particular time, I was so busy at the hospital—it probably saved me. I made up my mind I wasn't going to let it bother me. I also kept very busy with friends and social activities.

QUESTION: Your daughter, Lois, was fifteen then. What was it like for her to have her sixty-two-year-old father abruptly begin to fade away?

HARRIET: It wasn't a problem. Joe had always loved Lois, but he was never directly involved in raising her. Lois and I were very close, and she loved her father, but the family scene didn't change that much.

QUESTION: Did your friends start the I-told-you-so's when they saw what had happened to Joe?

HARRIET: No, but they didn't understand why I stayed with him. Several of my friends divorced their older husbands when they slowed down or became impotent. Joe found me when I was twenty-seven, unmarried, and not sure what I was going to do with my life. He gave me so much support in those early years, I figured I would help him out when he needed it.

QUESTION: Did you consider having an affair?

HARRIET: Oh, yes. I talked it over with Joe, and he didn't care. But he didn't want to know anything about it. Eventually, a friend I'd known for a long time and I became lovers. We were very discreet, and our relationship lasted for years.

QUESTION: Do you think that having a lover stabilized your marriage?

HARRIET: Frankly, I don't think it made any real difference. My lover was not a man I ever considered being married to. Joe and I had such respect and caring for each other, that we went along just fine. I was able to find some momentary pleasure outside of the marriage, but I knew that was all it was.

QUESTION: After age sixty-five, did Joe slow down more?

HARRIET: Yes. He lost interest in travel and most kinds of social affairs.

QUESTION: Did you gripe at him about this?

HARRIET: Yes. This was the area where I had the most trouble. I love weekend trips and travel of any kind. But Joe said, "You've got a car, money, and plenty of friends—go ahead." He never cared where I went or how long I stayed as long as I came home afterwards.

And there were many other compensations. I took care of my work, and Joe took care of everything else. The bills were always paid, shopping done, house cleaned, meals prepared on time, and every morning Joe came in with my coffee and the newspaper. I was treated like a queen.

Joe's problems were not of this doing. He didn't choose to be retired, and he didn't want to be unhealthy. None of Joe's difficulties were serious enough to break up our marriage.

QUESTION: You lost some things, but you gained some. That made the difference?

HARRIET: Yes. I tried to explain that to my girlfriends. Most of them who abandoned their older husbands and found new ones didn't stay married very long.

QUESTION: Did the life you describe continue for eleven years until Joe's death?

HARRIET: Yes. Only in the last year was he severely limited. I've never regretted staying with him to the end.

QUESTION: Joe died when you were fifty-four. How have you adjusted to being alone these last four years?

HARRIET: These years have not been what I thought they would be.

I have been more lonesome and depressed than at any other time of my life. I expected that I would meet men and go out and have fun, but I haven't met anyone. I've found that single women my age are not sought socially. Men who were interested in me when I was married avoid me now. All my widowed friends are going through the same thing.

One thing I did to cope with my loneliness was to invite one of my dearest friends to be my housemate. In fact, she came to live with us just before Joe passed away.

QUESTION: How has that worked out?

HARRIET: It's been very comforting, of course, but I suspect that her presence has slowed down my developing some men friends. I believe Joe was enormously relieved to know that I wasn't going to be alone after he was gone. I have so many friends, but I could be surrounded with people and still miss having a special man in my life.

QUESTION: What are you going to do about improving the male side of your social life?

HARRIET: I've been trying some things. I went to several singles groups, but I saw no one attractive to me. I've resisted the bar scene. After a party I go home alone, and I hate it. I'm open to the possibility of another marriage, though frankly I'd rather just live with an appropriate man. It would be much better for me financially.

QUESTION: What age range do you prefer in men friends now?

HARRIET: About my age.

QUESTION: What about finding a younger man?

HARRIET: I don't think so. I'd be afraid of getting a man so full of energy and pep that I couldn't keep up with him. That would bother me terribly. I'm at a stage of my life where I want to slow down a bit, and my man should be able to fit in with that.

QUESTION: What about having short-term lovers?

HARRIET: If I really liked a man—maybe. For some reason I'm being more fussy now about the quality of men I'd be interested in than ever before in my life. I don't know why. Occasionally men ask me out, and I sometimes turn them down. After all, I have a stable life with many options open to me. I don't have to do anything I don't want to. I suppose I'm a romantic. I'm waiting for the man with whom everything "clicks" when we meet. I'm trying to make myself available in many settings so that this will happen.

QUESTION: Are you optimistic about the future?

HARRIET: I think I am. My fussiness about men now proves that. If a man doesn't come into my life, I know that I have many good times ahead with my women friends.

QUESTION: Do you have any advice for people contemplating an age-different marriage?

HARRIET: If I had it all to do over again, I would do it—if the man were JOE. Some of my girlfriends are married to older men I couldn't spend five minutes with. It all depends on the man, not the age. Some men are over the hill at fifty-seven, and others are all washed up at twenty-seven. I would rather be alone than to choose the wrong mate—at any age.

One of the most serious problems of an age-different relationship is the integration of one partner into the life of the children of the other partner. Step-parenting is a notoriously difficult role. Being a stepchild may also be hazardous. Our next interviewee, Tina, was hazardous to her father's age-different marriage.

Tina was raised in a small town in Kentucky. Her father, a self-employed plumber, lived a precarious business life, and money was always scarce. Disgruntled, her mother worked part time, clerking in a variety store, and the family always seemed unsettled to Tina.

Tina had been born with a heart defect, and her ongoing health problems were another burden for the family to bear. A simple case of flu meant staying up all night to give Tina alcohol baths to prevent any fever. A fever would overwork Tina's weak heart, and might mean her death.

At age five, Tina's heart was repaired surgically, but the costs involved were a burden for many years. When she was eight, Tina remembers lying in her bed at night and listening to the muted sounds of her parents' battles.

Tina's parents separated when she was fourteen, and the limited family life she had collapsed. With an assist from tranquilizers, Tina's mother began to work full time, and Tina took over the parenting of her younger brother and sister.

The separation lasted a year, and hard feelings mounted. Tina's mother shifted all household responsibilities to Tina, started a social life of her own, and fought off visitation efforts by Tina's father. Finally the children fled to their father's house, and a divorce followed. Tina's mother moved to another state.

For two years Tina ran her father's household. It was a happier scene, but morning-to-evening work. Tina was finishing high school, experimenting with drugs, and dating men several years older than she. She said, "I became an adult instantly. All my friends were older, and I had to be a mother to my little brother and sister. I kept the family together."

When Tina was seventeen, her father, forty-four, became involved with a young woman of eighteen. Here is Tina talking about this critical event.

My father started dating a waitress from a cafe outside of town. Jill acted and looked older than her age, but I suspect she was a virgin. I liked her—she was the same age as many of my friends. I suspected, however, that, in part, she thought of my father as a way to get free of her parents. Dad set it up so Jill and I could spend an afternoon together, as we talked girl to girl. She told me she loved my father, but was afraid of sexual contact. I wasn't a virgin, and felt a lot older than Jill at that point.

Within a few weeks, Dad told us he was going to marry Jill. It was okay with all of us. Her family liked the youthfulness of my Dad, and didn't resist. When Dad and Jill came home from the honeymoon, everybody was uncertain about their roles.

Right away I resented the loss of my status as female head of the household. Jill took over everything. Trouble was, she was a terrible cook and inexperienced at all the work.

Dad and Jill got along fine. He had wanted somebody for a long time. There were a lot of embarrassing moments when Jill was mistaken for my sister. Jill tried to be things she wasn't and didn't know how to be—like a mother figure to me. I backed away fast.

Dad never complained about Jill's inexperience. He loved to teach her things, and she always responded to him. Jill found ways to bring things up, and I learned that she and Dad got along fine in bed. Jill wanted to use me for a confidant, like a girlfriend, and that was difficult for me. Jill was jealous of my social life, and uneasy with Dad any time a pretty girl was in the house.

Jill competed with us for Dad's attention. She began to be more critical of the way I lived my life. My dad gave me a lot of freedom, and Jill tried to be strict with me.

During the second year of Dad's marriage, my brother quit school, ran away from home, and never came back. Dad found himself more and more in the mediator role between Jill and me. Dad and Jill started quarrelling.

I began college and Jill, who had never even finished high school, became even more critical and demanding of me. Dad took me back as more of a confidant, and sometimes I even helped Dad and Jill settle an argument. That led to more jealousy from Jill.

Dad became very concerned because Jill had developed a circle of friends her own age, and he considered most of them unsavory. He decided to move out in the country, away from that scene, and I got an apartment close to school. It was also his backhand way of getting me out of the house and away from my constant hassles with Jill. Dad's decision was a kind of nice way out of a bad situation.

Later, after the move, Dad told me that troubles with Jill increased so much that she would go home to her parents for a few days to cool off. That amazed me, because she hated her home scene so much. Jill and Dad seemed to have no ability to solve problems.

Dad said that as Jill got a little older, a more independent, critical side of her nature surfaced, and the only way they could deal with their differences was to separate for a while. This pattern became habitual.

Eventually Jill stayed away for months at a time, and while she was gone she started dating other men. Part of Dad and Jill's problem was that they had never developed any supportive friendships with other couples. They stayed to themselves. There was no friend or family support available to either of them.

I don't think they're going to make it. Loneliness and dependency bring them back to each other periodically, but eventually each will find a solution for that elsewhere. Dad's needs are still the same, but Jill is in a totally different phase from where she was when they married four years ago. Their marriage is doomed.

Divorce is almost always the ultimate slayer of a relationship. A few, but not many, couples survive that devastating development. Pam's age-different marriage did not survive. As a way of meeting the final interviewee of this chapter, I want to share with you the notes that Jesalee made as I prepared to tape-record Pam's remarks.

We have found that tape-recorded conversations, when listened to much later, offer a disembodied voice, and if our memories fail —no visual images. For that reason, as I set up our recording equipment, Jesalee makes notes on the person and the setting. Here is what she wrote about Pam.

> Beautiful, expensive home, tastefully furnished. A maid is cleaning while we are there. Pam is attractive, acts thirty-five, but looks younger. Short blonde hair, pale skin, slender. Chain smokes. Orders Valium from pharmacy while Jack is setting up. Very bright, alive demeanor, and clearly comfortable as she talks to us. Pam has a punchy, aggressive style of speaking. A bit abrasive at times. Too early to be sure, but I got a sense of anger, defensiveness, and perhaps hostility just beneath her smile.

Pam is forty. She has been married to Pat, fifty-eight, for nineteen years. They have two daughters, fifteen and seventeen, and Pam and Pat are in the process of getting divorced.

Pat wouldn't talk to us, and Pam talked too much. For nearly three hours we sat, helpless to guide her, while she poured out histories, memories, anecdotes, and her philosophy of life. Her word picture painted the classic scene of opposite types being attracted to each other. Emotional, demonstrative, outspoken, giddy Pam and taciturn, stable, intellectual, low-key Pat—they are the All-American couple. Psychiatrists write articles about this particular pair and what they get from each other.

Pam and Pat met in a military setting, and Pam, like a newly commissioned lieutenant, conducted their courtship as a kind of war game. Pam was raised as an "Air Force brat," and she knew about these matters. With her father, the general, and her mother, the very stuffy general's wife, Pam had lived on more than twenty-one air bases during her first twenty-one years.

Pam's father wore the mantle of strictness, and her mother personified propriety, and neither related well to their only daughter. They nearly disowned her when Pam became pregnant at sixteen. In those days, abortion was out of the question, and though Pam was willing, the families ruled against marriage to her high school sweetheart.

Pam spent several months in a home for unwed mothers—a pseudonym for a reform school. There, abandoned by her family and lover, she waited for, gave birth to, and gave up for adoption her child. Pam feels scarred by that teenage experience, and she tells of wandering the streets in the neighborhood of the adoption home in hopes of a glimpse of her baby.

Pain passes, and during the summer of her twenty-first year Pam was with her parents following her third year at a university. A toothache took her to Pat.

Pat started out as a Nebraska farm boy, and years of education and professional experience have only diluted his midwestern background. The middle son in a large family, hard work and the professional boost of World War II launched him on a career as a dentist in the Air Force. A short, unhappy marriage in his early thirties did not slow his professional development, but made him perpetually wary of women.

Pam looked up from Pat's dental chair and decided he was the man for her. That he was thirty-nine did not enter as a factor in her planning. Pam mounted her attack with precision. First there was a barrage of notes, funny cards, and spicy telephone calls to soften him up. Then she arranged to be in the right spots to run into him.

When Pat offered no dates, Pam escalated the attack to the next phase. She arranged to be invited on group outings with Pat's friends. After two dozen of these indirect dates, Pam took an apartment a few doors from Pat to keep an eye on him. Within six months, Pat proposed (capitulated), and a few weeks later they were married.

A few days after the wedding, Pam and Pat were sent to a remote Air Force communications station in Greenland. Their eight months in that isolated setting formed the patterns that remained with them the rest of their married life. Pam played the petulant, spoiled brat, and Pat the stable, loving father.

When life got tough in the cold and ice and Pam threatened to go home, Pat said, "Go!" Pam threw a temper tantrum, and when Pat didn't respond, she decided to stay.

In their third and fifth years of marriage, daughters Lisa and Kim were born. Pat left the military in their seventh year, and his private practice soared almost immediately.

In their tenth year of marriage, Pat and Pam presented themselves to a marriage counselor for assistance. He listened awhile and said to Pat, "You need to have this person who will look up to you with adoring eyes and ask for your wisdom." To Pam, the counselor remarked, "You have a lot of traits Pat admires—traits he doesn't have."

The marriage counselor put his finger on the pulse of their marriage and revealed the father-daughter nature of it. Pat and Pam suspected he was right. Their sex life had been terrible. Pam had never had an orgasm. She claimed Pat had plenty of "fatherly warmth," but no passion.

Pat started to worry that he was slowing down, but Pam insisted that he had never been a very active person.

And so their marriage staggered on. The final collapse of the union between Pam and Pat was triggered by their older daughter, Lisa. Raising her had been a hellish affair, and her adolescence was a nightmare. After Lisa had gone through extended bouts with drugs and three abortions, Pam decided to move out of the family home.

Pat had blamed Lisa's troubles on Pam's child-rearing techniques, and the constant conflict in the home had become insufferable. Pam left, saying, "If I'm the problem, I'll get out of the way and we'll see what happens."

For a while the house was calmer, "but only because Pat is a very permissive parent," Pam says. Eventually, Pat engineered the departure of Lisa, then eighteen, and buried himself in his work. Three years of attempted reconciliations were followed by a divorce action. Pam moved in and out of their home several times. She took a job in a nearby town and began to develop her own life. She found a lover and effortlessly experienced orgasms. And she nurtured her anger toward Pat.

Now Pam has the family home, where she lives with her younger daughter. A property settlement guarantees her financial future. As we talked, she reviewed the list of Pat's limitations: he would never fight; he would not discuss sex; he worked too much; he treated her like a child; he had few friends, and the ones he had were older colleagues with dull wives; and he ignored the children.

Pat lives alone in a small apartment, and says he is looking for romance and warmth.

Pam wants a man at least ten years her junior, because she believes that her personality fits better with younger people.

In this chapter I've introduced you to many of the losers in age-different relationships. The people you met were mostly big-time losers. There is another large group of small-time losers, who are much more difficult to identify and locate.

There are those age-different couples who are doing all right with each other, but have never quite managed the world around them. These couples often lead very cloistered lives. With few friends and limited public exposure as couples, they struggle with their self-doubts.

Recently I stood in a long line at the airport waiting to board a plane. An elderly woman and a young man walked by holding hands, and, like a wave washing along a beach, every head in the line turned as they passed. After the couple was gone, the conversation level of the people in the line intensified, discussing, I suppose, the nature of the couple's connection.

Endless versions of this kind of public attention are unnerving and sometimes damaging to many age-different couples. Ordinary cases of mistaken identity cause overreactions, which confuse and embarrass innocent people. Of course it does become tiresome for a husband to be identified as a father, son, nephew, or uncle, for example.

There are more biting versions that lie beyond simple mistaken identity. Here are a few I've collected for the man-older couple:

"That's your *husband?*"

"What's it like living with that old guy?"

"Is that old fellow any good in bed?"

"If you're married to *him*—here's my telephone number."

"I bet you married him for his money."

"Looking for a father?"

"You must have been desperate!"

Each of you can imagine a woman-older scenario to accompany the previous comments. Couples who learn how to deal with these pressures are strengthened and their relationships thrive. Others falter and fail.

CHAPTER TEN

Is an Age-Different Relationship for You?

W**HAT** DO YOU think? After reading about the experiences of so many people, do you want to try an age-different relationship? Or perhaps you are in one and you would like to understand it better in the hope of enriching the interaction even more.

If you read the interviews carefully, some basic ideas about age-different mating practices fairly jumped from the page. The uncensored perceptions of bold people experiencing a unique life adventure can guide us to clearer understanding of age-different unions. There is a strong practical flavor in age-different relationships. Recall that the words "phase" and "stage" kept popping up. And people mentioned again and again their "needs," and what they wanted from their partners.

A straightforward combination of these words from the interviews and their implied ideas leads to these statements:

- Two people are attracted to each other, in a romantic or friendly way, by a sense of liking bolstered by the perception that each has things to offer that the other wants.
- The attraction begins the relationship, but the exchange of needs sustains it.
- The quality of mutual gratification depends on the development of the individuals involved. That development is called "stage."

In our culture it is rare for anyone to make the stormy voyage through life without hearing someone grumble: "Act your age!" Taken out of context, the precise meaning of the message is uncertain. The implication is clear, however. The accuser is insisting that the accused possesses a particular chronological age, and that his or her behavior does not relate appropriately to that age. Sometimes it is not clear what actions are being faulted, and frequently the suitable standard of behavior for the age is hazy.

The details of the expletive are usually not important. This societal slander loosely discredits a person's functioning at a certain time and place. Whether the functioning involves lifting a large box, remembering a telephone number, talking too much, or getting a suitable job is of little importance. With three little words, one's stage of development is discredited.

Individuals carry versions of the age-stage model around in their heads. When these images are collected, society's standards are revealed. What all this means is that, on the average, given a specified age, people in our culture are expected to act and to be able to perform in a certain way. It's not clear whether the expectations of developmental stages came from observations over the years, or were intellectually formed as reasonable and appropriate goals for an age. Probably some of both.

The result is that for every age there is a real or imagined developmental stage which presumes some specific achievement with physical, social, and personal dimensions. What was really being said was, "Act your stage!"

Intuitively, we all know about stage. When we say, "She's a late bloomer," or "He's in his second childhood," we are sensing a gap between developmental stage and chronological age. Many researchers studied the relatively uncomplicated lives of children. They identified the stages between birth and adolescence. So precise are these stages that tests can show exactly where a child is on this path of development.

With adults it's much more difficult. Only in recent years have our social scientists studied adult stages, and most of the basic concepts of adult development remain unknown. The most impressive work on the subject has been done by Daniel Levinson of Yale and presented in his book, *The Seasons of a Man's Life.* I use the adjective "impressive," and yet this seminal effort studied the lives of only forty people—all male and middle class. George Vaillant, in his *Adaptation to Life,* wrote: ·

> Humans are not mature at Freud's five or Saint Loyola's seven or even the law's 18 or 21. Ronald Reagan's ultra-liberal college politics must seem utterly foreign to him now; for one price of growing up is to lose touch with one's past.

And later he continued:

> Certainly there is nothing magical about a given year; Elliott Jacque's thirty-seven, Gail Sheehy's "Catch 30," Daniel Levinson's forty-to-forty-two definitions of middle life crisis are as arbitrary as suggesting that adolescent crises occur at sixteen.[1]

Gail Sheehy combed the work of Levinson and others, and in *Passages* constructed a developmental ladder of six stages for adults. But here's the rub. The stages have fuzzy beginnings and ends, they are loosely described, and an individual's unique experience in a stage cannot be predicted.

In order to understand how age-different couples get together, we must learn more about stages. Is a successful union formed by couples at the same stage, or are there complementary stages that fit together best? And what aspects of personal development are most critical for age-different mate selection?

When two people meet, each person brings some degree of physical, social, personal, intellectual, and spiritual development to the interaction. The extent of the development of an attribute of each person depends on heredity and life experiences. Age may influence the extent of a particular kind of development, but not necessarily. We've all seen old men with young bodies and very young children who can sing and dance like adult professionals.

If two people spend some time together, each (often without being conscious of it) gets an idea about the development of the other person. That's *perceived maturity*. Then, depending on the attraction between the people and how willing each is to try to satisfy his or her desires, some kind of coupling may occur. Nowhere in this description is age a necessary factor. The interaction depends on the values, needs, attitudes, and goals that are a part of any developmental stage. Scientists study the battle between the inner and outer self. They compare behavior that is motivated by inner yearnings to actions that are a consequence of what the world expects people to do. Age-different couples, more than most, are moved by perceived inner forces.

Why people are attracted to one another seems incredibly complex. As I read the theories, one of them comes through clearly: If people are acting instinctively, the issue of age doesn't come up. The age-different relationship is a natural union.

Actress Jeanne Moreau said in a recent interview:

There's a magic about numbers. Thirty, forty, fifty . . . it's been imposed by the culture. All those rules about who you can love and who you can't love and how. Since I was a little girl I've been violently opposed to rules. Why should I deprive myself of my adventure, which is my life, of going through something for the first time because perhaps I am not twenty anymore? Why should I defer to society in that way? [2]

Moreau has touched on a key issue. We may view developmental stages as one of our culture's ways of controlling us—of putting limits on our behavior. An imagined cultural axiom might go something like this: "Keep people near the behavioral norm and the culture will be more stable." Or we can think of developmental stages as naturally occurring phenomena. Understanding them will give us guidance on the conduct of our lives. The second view offers a more positive outlook; in addition, the sting of the social stigma attached to age-different unions has been reduced significantly. If we understand stages better, our chances of choosing more suitable mates improve.

There are clues on how to proceed with increasing our understanding if we look at the way stages are characterized for school children. Years of study have produced vivid descriptions of behavior in the physical, social, emotional, and mental dimensions of children.[3] For example, the physical development of a youngster in the primary grades is described as: "Active; large-muscle control; eye development incomplete; susceptible to illnesses; accident rate at peak." In elementary grades the social development is characterized by: "Interested in gangs; sex differences; team games; hero worship." If we inquire about the emotional development of a junior high school student, the answer will be: "Moody, unpredictable; temperamental; may be opinionated and intolerant; critical of adults." The stage of mental development of a high school student is portrayed as: "Close to maximum mental efficiency but inexperienced; a philosophy of life and sense of identity. Conflicts over sex role and occupational identity."

Anyone who has spent time with children will recognize how invalid these terse descriptions may be. Their intent is to pinpoint the most important commonly occurring maturation characteristics of children so that suitable educational programs can be designed. Beyond these key factors of emotional, social, mental, and physical development lie the details necessary to write a school curriculum or design a reading program.

No such specificity of intent exists for adult developmental stages. No finer picture of the dramatic events of life and the details of living has been possible. There is no single stage of a person's life that can be understood separately from the events that precede it and the outcomes that follow it.

Aging is three ongoing processes—biological, psychological, and social. These processes interact with each other and the environment, both physical and cultural, to shape the life an individual experiences. For adults there are many indications of stage—maturity milestones such as working full time or parenthood. These milestones create sets of needs. It is impossible to be very specific about the overall developmental stage of a large group of thirty-five-year-old female adults without considering needs. A thirty-five-year-old woman may be psychologically thirty-five (she is responsible, has high self-esteem, and has a zest for life) but socially eighteen (she is living at home, has trouble keeping friends, and is still in school) and biologically sixty-five (she has very low energy and a chronic heart condition). Her "variable maturity" creates a unique set of needs for her.

All of us bring our stages to relationships as we try to determine who, or what kind of person, will bring us pleasure. Some of us choose partners because of characteristics like beauty or wealth, and the outcome is often grievous. Most people, however, select relationships based on a desire to satisfy needs.

The needs approach requires that we know what our needs are; that we understand the needs of another person; and that we have a basis of mixing or matching our respective stages to form relationships that will mutually satisfy the needs.

There is a great deal of data to support the idea that stage—not age—is an important part of selecting a mate. For many reasons I've discussed, a person may choose not to pay attention to developmental stage, or not know how to use the ideas. While not a panacea, the stage approach offers rational guidance to mate selection. If one is madly in love at the outset of a relationship, it may be difficult to be rational, but a long-term awareness of your partner's stage will contribute to the richness and stability of your relationship.

The question of whether we choose mates "like us" or "opposite us" is a spurious issue. We do both—depending on our constellation of needs. "Opposites attract" and "like attracts like" are two ends of a continuum along which the goal is to *balance the stages and needs* in order to form a happy, stable union between two people.

When people seek "similars" to form relationships, the kinds of factors they consider are: age, race, religion, ethnic origin, location of previous residence, social class, economic status, education, and previous marital status. Later screening for personality and temperament characteristics narrows the choice. The attempt, of course, is to guarantee the quality of the future union, but there are many uncertainties. Comparing information of this sort often has little to do with the interpersonal dynamics of forming a relationship. If two people plan a marriage based on matching backgrounds without considering developmental stage—anything can happen.

Selection factors listed above function often only to form a group of eligibles from which, for example, a person may choose a spouse. Next, we have to consider what we mean by "falling in love." First, there is a complex attraction called "romantic love," followed by another kind of love that expresses the individual's further needs beyond romantic love. The relationship evolves so that each partner can find a wide range of gratification through interaction with the other.

To keep the range of topics manageable, I will focus on mate selection leading to heterosexual age-different marriage. In our culture the choice of mates is voluntary, and premarital interaction between men and women is encouraged as a kind of testing of potential mates. The needs I've mentioned frequently refer to physical and social needs. There is ample evidence to prove that needs influence perceptions. The stronger our needs, the more we tune in to our environment to find a situation that will gratify our needs. The classic textbook example is of the physician and his wife in bed: his wife awakens to the cry of the baby as he sleeps on; he awakens to the ring of the telephone, and her sleep is undisturbed.

To use stage as a basis of mate selection, let's assume for the moment that an individual is capable of perceiving himself and his potential spouse in rich detail. That is, he can perceive his own needs and estimate the capability of his potential partner to gratify those needs—and vice versa. First, of course, what are the specific needs? Social scientists often describe them in this way:

1. *Achievement*—to work hard to create something and/or emulate others.
2. *Sociability*—to come near and enjoy contact with one or more people.
3. *Independence*—to avoid or escape domination or control.
4. *Compliance*—to yield or defer to other people.
5. *Dominance*—to influence and control the behavior of other people.

6. *Humiliation*—to invite, seek, or accept blame or criticism from oneself or others.
7. *Hostility*—to fight, injure, or kill others.
8. *Nurturance*—to give sympathy and aid to a weak, helpless, ill, or dejected person.
9. *Recognition*—to invoke the admiration and approval of others.
10. *Succor*—to be helped, loved, protected, or indulged by people.[4]

Perhaps you can think of more. Consider this a limited list suitable for examples and discussion.

It's important to separate needs from personality traits such as passivity, anxiousness, and sexiness. Presumably, partners consider these traits during early stages of attraction.

Let's see how these needs function in mate selection. We can do this by a series of questions and answers.

Who wants a hostile person? Someone who enjoys humiliation.

Who wants a person who needs assistance? Someone who likes to nurture.

Who wants a person who needs constant recognition? Someone who likes to defer.

These simplistic matchings of opposites shield the inherent complexity of the need-pairs. A man may want a woman to be independent at home and dependent in public. A woman may want nurturing—but not a lot.

What about the matching of couples with similar needs? Presumably they can get together if their need intensities are very different. For example, a highly dominant man should find a woman with little need to dominate. A woman who needs a great deal of nurturing would be more comfortable with a man who doesn't need much.

Looking at needs satisfaction is a way to begin to predict the future success of an age-different union. Needs are a consequence of the stage of a person, not the age. The trouble is that rarely are interactions as easy to follow as the triangle of Joe, Mary, and Betty. Joe, fifty-one, is acquainted with Mary, twenty-eight, and Betty, thirty-one. Joe is a dominant man and is fairly intolerant of others' viewpoints. Mary is very like Joe, but Betty is easily influenced by others and usually defers to their wishes. Joe is likely to choose Betty for a relationship, because he sees her as a "truly feminine, tractable, agreeable young lady who knows when and how to help a man." To Betty, Joe is "a tower of strength." On the other hand, Joe would turn away from Mary and see her as "bossy, unfeminine, and shrewish."

Real people, not contrived examples, are likely to have several need-pairs, both opposite and similar, operating at different levels of intensity. We need to go further to account for more realistic conditions. Don't misunderstand, however—mixing and matching needs have already given us an interesting and useful way to look at ourselves and others, and a basis of speculation on the promise of developing close age-different relationships.

Refinements are needed to make the mixing and matching of the needs approach more useful. We must have a way of learning how strong or weak a person's needs may be; how needs of different strengths can form pairs; and how we can account for several need-pairs operating simultaneously.

In order to respond to the first issue, let's delve more deeply into an individual's perceptive capabilities. The most meaningful index of a stage is the individual's perceived age. When someone says, "I feel like being babied," or "You look like you need a friend today," he is perceiving a state that may be valid only at that moment. Most people, either intuitively or with guidance, can perceive their own or another's needs. It is perceived needs, a part of perceived maturity, that are the key to mixing and matching developmental stages in order to form age-different couples.

"Perceived needs" sounds very technical and foreboding, but it isn't. It's a very natural activity occurring almost automatically, and we want to take a close look at it. All of us routinely observe body posture, facial expressions, voice tone, and the like to get a sense of what is going on with people. We watch individuals with other people, see them a little drunk, and note how they behave when they are very tired. By dozens of different ways we gather information about the people we want to involve in our lives.

Eventually we allow individuals to come closer to us. Then, as interaction intensifies, we gather other information about them.

Our experience and intuition allow us to score, weigh, and combine these perceptions to create our personal sense of an individual. It can be amazingly accurate.

People often ignore, or don't believe, their perceptions of others. Some people may prefer to read a resumé or ask friends, but only old, uncertain information can be gathered in this way.

Perceived needs are constantly modifying and changing—sometimes quickly and other times slowly—as a development stage evolves. The potential complexity is staggering. Imagine two people relating to each other while combinations of need-pairs pass through transitions. How do we peel away the complexity? The major prerequisite is a reasonably sensitive normal person.

We can get a better feel for the idea of perceived needs by first looking at a parallel example—perceived health. Simply ask someone how he or she feels at that moment, and request that the answer be given in the form of a number between one and ten, where zero is death and ten is the pinnacle of healthiness. Most people, after a few seconds' pause, will give a number.

Try it on yourself right now. How are you today? Was your answer 5, or 8—or perhaps the scale was too coarse, and you chose a 6.5?

Now stop and think what the number you chose means. It is the result of an internalized assessment of every aspect of your life that contributes to your feeling of healthiness. That includes your body, emotions, spirit, friends, work, and so on. Each facet of your life was evaluated, then combined with the other parts according to your primary values to create, within a few seconds, a measure of your perceived health.

You may ask, "But does the number mean anything? If I had lost my job the day before, wouldn't that reduce my score even though I was in perfect physical condition? And if I had a latent deadly disease, might I not have a high score now and die a month later?"

The answer to both questions is yes. The score is your subjective evaluation of your health status at a particular moment. To get a better feeling for the score you gave, visualize this scenario: After I receive your answer, a group of experts who have been waiting in the wings will descend upon you. Physicians, psychiatrists, and behavioral scientists of all persuasions will examine and test you. They might require a complete physical fitness testing, psychological examinations, and the like. When they finish their work, a professional group meeting will be held to combine their individual findings. When their wrangling ceases and agreement is reached, days and thousands of dollars later, research has shown that, on the average, the platoon of experts would merely confirm your two-second self-assessment.[5] The point is, of course, that no one is more capable of knowing about you than you. Similarly, your available—and latent—powers of perception and intuition can be directed at others as well as at yourself. In order to use your natural powers to assist in forming age-different relationships, you must *develop the ability, through increased awareness, to perceive needs.*

First impressions of people are a powerful and valuable experience, although we may forget, ignore, discredit, or not notice them. The amazing ability of an individual to know a great deal, in a very short time, on apparently little information, about another person is available to all of us.

Many researchers have experimented with people to study their perceptive powers. A simple test is to allow an individual to mingle socially for a few minutes with ten strangers. Then the individual is instructed to give, either written or orally, every detail of his first impression of each of the ten strangers. The information that can be detected by many observers is significantly accurate.

We use perceptive powers to evaluate our own and another person's needs. I asked Don and Lucy to provide the scores for this example. They have a twenty-one-year age difference, and have been married for two and one-half years. First they looked at the list of needs, and each chose and scored on a scale of 10, a needs list for each person. They were told to include any important needs not on my list. Here are the first results of their perceptions:

(D)	Don	(L)	(D)	Lucy	(L)
8	Achievement	0	3	Achievement	5
5	Sociability	4	9	Sociability	7
9	Independence	7	–	Independence	4
			7	Compliance	–
6	Dominance	8			
7	Nurturance	7	6	Nurturance	8
–	Recognition	4			
4	Succor	8	10	Succor	8
			–	Monogamy	9

Both agreed that Achievement was a need for both—high for Don and mid-range for Lucy. Lucy thought that Achievement was more important for her than Don perceived it, and that involved a lively discussion about what kind of achievement Lucy wanted. Don saw Lucy as wanting to be more sociable than she perceived herself. They compromised on a score of 8 for Lucy. Don was only 50-50 in sociability. Don scored high in Independence, though he thought he needed more freedom than Lucy perceived. Don didn't even list Independence as a need for Lucy, even though she scored herself a 4. Lucy explained to Don what independence meant to her.

Compliance was scored in a complicated way. Only Don scored as needing compliance. I pointed out Don's high scores in Dominance and described alternate definitions of Compliance. After some thought, Lucy gave herself 5 in Compliance.

Lucy's and Don's needs for Nurturance were fairly high. They seemed to be very giving people. Their needs to receive help were appropriately counterbalanced, except for Lucy's sense that Don wanted a great deal of Succor. Lucy noted Don's need for Recognition and her own intense desire for a monogamous relationship. Don listed neither of these. Apparently marital fidelity had been inferred, but never discussed, so they talked about it.

After the silent scoring of perceived needs by Lucy and Don, followed by discussion and compromise, the needs list and scores looked like this:

NEEDS

Don		Lucy
9	Achievement	4
4	Sociability	8
8	Independence	4
2	Compliance	6
8	Dominance	2
7	Nurturance	7
4	Recognition	1
5	Succorance	9

Simply going through the exercise of developing this list was an eye-opening experience for both Don and Lucy. Both said that they had known, in a different form, most of the information, but that many blank spots were filled in. Forming the list caused them to talk about matters never before discussed.

The original lists developed separately and silently by Don and Lucy could be used by either of them as an assessment of the relationship without involving the other person. Clues as to the promise of a budding age-different romance might be obtained in this way. Or perceived needs are a way to monitor an age-different couple as they change stages during a long-term relationship.

Recall that the needs list is evaluated by looking for very different scores in the same need, and the same scores in opposite needs. For example, Don's need to dominate is balanced by Lucy's low score in Dominance and fairly high score in Compliance. Monogamy is interpreted as a characteristic of the couple, and thus is not treated as a need.

One more step can assist Don and Lucy in using perceived needs to check the health of their age-different relationship. The fact that not all needs are of equal importance to an individual can be accounted for in the assessment of the matching. If three needs were listed and scored as the critical factors by an age-different couple, then I'd ask them which need was most important. The man might say that all three needs were of equal importance to him. On the other hand, the woman could insist that the first need is twice as important as either of the other two. The individual's values regarding needs are revealed by my questioning, and can be accounted for by adjusting the scores.

An easy way to do this is to ask each partner to divide one hundred points among the needs in the list so that the most important needs receive more points. In this simple manner each need is weighted by a percentage equivalent to the value that need has to the individual.

I asked Don and Lucy, each working separately, to divide one hundred points among the needs on their list. Here are the results:

NEED

Don			Lucy	
Points	*Score*		*Points*	*Score*
15	9	Achievement	10	4
10	4	Sociability	25	8
15	8	Independence	10	4
10	2	Compliance	10	6
15	8	Dominance	10	2
15	7	Nurturance	10	7
10	4	Recognition	0	1
10	5	Succor	25	9

When I asked Don how he assigned his points, he said, "I chose the four most important needs on the list, decided they were of equal importance to me, and that together they were worth more than half all the points. In that way I gave fifteen points to Achievement, Independence, Dominance, and Nurturance. I split the remaining points equally among the other four needs."

Lucy described her arithmetic in this way: "Sociability and Succor mean more to me than anything—so I split half the points between them. The other needs, except for Recognition, were about the same to me, so I divided the fifty remaining points among them."

If you had added the needs score without any adjustment for importance (that means all needs would be considered of equal importance), the difference between Lucy's and Don's perceived needs would have been 15 percent. After accounting for the importance of needs, the sum of the scores was separated by 4 percent. The perceived-needs method, as a form of age-different mate selection, suggests that the mix and match of needs looks good for Don and Lucy, and that since the sums of each partner's importance-adjusted scores are similar, the prospects for the successful union of the couple are good.

I want to summarize the use of perceived needs as a basis for choosing an age-different partner or evaluating an age-different couple. Basically, the approach involves answering a series of questions until some useful guidance is achieved. These results are intended to assist, not replace, any other means an individual has for choosing an age-different mate. Here are the questions, with some follow-up comments:

1. What are my needs and those of my potential or existing partner? Using one's powers of perception, a list of needs unique to the individual and a separate list unique to the partner is formed. It is important to differentiate between traits and needs. If you must have a tall, dark, and handsome man, presumably that requirement is already met in forming your group of eligible partners. A simple way to separate needs and traits is to remember that a need requires the exchange of human energy. If you want to be whipped once a week, that's a need; if you require a partner with an I.Q. of at least 150, that's a trait. The needs list must be very specific and personalized. If you do not believe you are a particularly perceptive person, I've listed several sources in the chapter references which will help you tune your powers of perception.

2. What are the strengths of my perceived needs and those of my mate? The intuitive awareness of the intensity of a need can be scored easily by most people. If you suspect your powers of awareness are minimal, read some of the books I've given in the chapter references.

3. What is the quality of the mix and match of need-pairs? If a need-pair involves the same need, the scores should be very different for successful mating. For a need-pair containing complementary needs, desirable scores should be near the same magnitude. If there are few need-pairs in existence between the couple, that is, if one person has a need for which the other has neither a similar nor a complementary need, the future of the relationship may be dim.

4. How important is each need? It is necessary to differentiate between the intensity of a need and the importance of a need. Imagine a man who needs a lot of support from his wife. Each morning before he leaves for work, she gives him plenty of physical and emotional loving to prepare him for the day. He has come to expect her efforts and accepts them as a part of their marriage. The same man, on the average of once every six months, needs a pat on the back from his boss. Without his boss's recognition, the man's morale crumbles. This man's perceived needs for succor will score very high, but his wife's support is taken for granted and not very important in his life. On the other hand, he doesn't need very much reinforcement from his boss, but what little he gets is incredibly important to him.

5. *How does importance influence the evaluation of perceived needs?* The division of 100 points among the needs which have been listed offers the possibility of adjusting the impact of each need on the summation of the scores for the perceived need. Multiply the number of points assigned to each perceived need by the score given to the same perceived need and sum those products. The closer the two sums, one for each person, the more promising the age-different union.

The five questions just reviewed are the basis of the perceived-needs approach to age-different mate selection. The method's key qualities are rationality and practicality. The approach assumes that people attracted to an age-different relationship have a somewhat less emotional approach to the interpersonal unions; that they have fairly high self-esteem; that a person's maturity is more important than age; that they are perceptive and intuitive people; and that what is happening in the present is more important than what is going to occur in the future.

"Wait," you may say, "I'm not sure I'm that sort of person. How can I know if an age-different relationship is right for me before I try one?" The answer to your question is that you must explore yourself with respect to the assumptions just given. To help with your self-investigation, I've devised a series of questions to determine your ADQ—your Age Difference Quotient. The higher your ADQ score, the more likely you are a candidate for an age-different relationship.

1. Do you frequenty feel uncomfortable with a person whose age is significantly different from yours?   Yes *No*
2. How many close friends do you have whose age differs from yours by at least fifteen years?   _____
3. If an older person in your life lost his/her money, power, position, or prestige, would that matter?   Yes *No*
4. Older men and women make better lovers because they know what younger people want.   Yes *No*
5. Did your parents fail to give you enough love and attention?   *Yes* No
6. Do you frequently get the feeling of wanting to be taken care of?   Yes *No*
7. Older people are more self-confident, aggressive, and dependable.   Yes *No*
8. Is it difficult for you to spend much time alone?   *Yes* No
9. Do you get bored easily?   *Yes* No
10. Do you have difficulty making simple decisions?   Yes *No*
11. Have you ever lied about your age?   Yes *No*
12. When you meet a new person, do you inquire about his/her age before very long?   Yes *No*
13. Do you find people your own age uninteresting?   *Yes* No
14. Is it difficult for you to spend much time with your parents?   *Yes* No
15. Is being in love more important than your career?   Yes *No*
16. Do you think much about the time when you will retire?   *Yes* No
17. Do you especially enjoy bumping into a former friend and spending a lot of time telling stories about the past?   *Yes* No
18. Do you always "act your age?"   Yes *No*
19. Do you sometimes wish you were more intelligent?   *Yes* No
20. Would you mind submitting to psychological testing?   Yes *No*
21. Do you have any serious health problems?   Yes *No*
22. Have you ever had any trouble with the law?   Yes *No*
23. Are you fifteen pounds overweight?   *Yes* No
24. Do new situations and people make you very anxious?   *Yes* No
25. Do you have any trouble sleeping?   *Yes* No
26. Is it difficult for you to concentrate?   *Yes* No

27. Do you have difficulty believing your intuitive flashes?
    Yes No

28. Is it difficult for you to trust your first impression of people?
    Yes No

29. Is it hard for you to receive compliments from someone?
    Yes No

30. Would you prefer to be significantly more self-confident?
    Yes No

31. Does change bother you very much?   Yes No

32. Are you easily embarrassed?   Yes No

33. Do you consider yourself an "overreactor?"   Yes No

34. Are you often depressed?   Yes No

35. Do you consider yourself a compulsive person?   Yes No

36. Has jealousy been an important issue in your life?   Yes No

37. Are you fearful of getting old?   Yes No

38. Do you often find yourself without enough energy for the day?
    Yes No

39. Is the permanence of a relationship a critical quality for you?
    Yes No

40. Is it difficult for you to imagine yourself in an age-different
    relationship?   Yes No

Score the questions in this way. Give +1 for every "no" answer, −1 for every "yes" response, and 0 for a "don't know" or "not sure" response. Then add the sum of these scores to the answer to question 2. If you are able to score over 30 points for the 40 questions, you will probably do well in age-different relationships.

The nature of the questions reveals the type of person who will be most inclined to age-different relationships. Visualize an individual like this: A man or woman who has high self-confidence and prefers to live life with a bit of practical flavor; someone capable of deep emotion, but with overtones of rationality; a perceptive, intuitive, aware person to whom the maturity of another person is very important; an individual who lives very much for the present. These characteristics describe many normal American men and women for whom age is not a factor. This does not mean, of course, that an eccentric, rich fifty-year-old man and a childish, sexy twenty-year-old woman cannot marry and successfully exchange favors. In mating practices anything is possible.

From interacting with many age-different couples over several years, I have distilled the several qualities that are common to the largest group of successful age-different mates. Possessing these attributes guarantees nothing, but suggests that on the average these people will enrich their lives with age-different relationships. Many others will, too.

The most valuable aspect of the perceived-needs approach and the ADQ for age-different mate selection is the nature of the dialogue they provoke. The exercises force potential partners to look at each other in special ways, and that mutual examination can help clear away the problems of age-difference stigma and self-doubt. Some couples may not be up to this kind of effort, but even a modest attempt can be rewarding. Even though needs may change with time and situation, paying attention to your own and your partner's needs may become a permanent part of your life.

Life enrichment is the theme of this book. A chronic national problem is the personal alienation of many of our citizens. Not letting age be a factor, and opening our lives to more people will help solve this problem. All of us have the genuine option of achieving more enriching relationships in our life by overcoming our agism limitations.

NOTES

CHAPTER 1: MAY-DECEMBER ROMANCES

1. Lee Tully, "My Favorite Jokes," *Sacramento Bee*, 21 August 1977.
2. Cited in Judy Stoffman, "Dr. Spock at 75," *The Atlanta Journal*, 3 March 1979.
3. Cited in Doug Grow, "Wilkinson Defies Age with St. Louis," *The Atlanta Constitution*, 15 May 1979.
4. Cited in Pete Axthelm, "A Voice from the South," *Newsweek* (31 January 1977), p. 25.
5. D. R. Reuben, "20-Year Itch," *Reader's Digest* (May 1975), pp. 79–82.
6. "*Time* Essay: In Praise of May-December Marriages," *Time* (21 February 1969), pp. 34–35.
7. Cited in *Time* Essay, p. 35.
8. Cited in Allen Young, *Gay Sunshine Interview* (Bolinas, Calif.: Grey Fox Press, 1974), p. 15.
9. Cited in *Time* Essay, p. 35.

CHAPTER 3: LET'S NOT REINVENT THE WHEEL

1. Bernard Murstein, *Love, Sex and Marriage through the Ages* (New York: Springer Publishing Co., 1974).
2. Robert Winch, *Mate Selection* (New York: Harper & Row, Publishers, 1958).
3. Cited in Murstein, p. 223.
4. Murstein, p. 238.
5. William Congreve, *The Way of the World,* act 4, scene 1.
6. Cited in Thomas Monahan, *The Pattern of Age at Marriage in the United States,* vol. 2 (Philadelphia: Stephanson Brothers, 1951), p. 296.
7. Cited in Monahan, p. 310.
8. Cited in Monahan, p. 312.
9. J. R. Udry, *The Social Context of Marriage* (New York: J. B. Lippincott Co., 1966), p. 317.

CHAPTER 4: A DIFFERENT KIND OF MARRIAGE

1. Bernard Murstein, *Love, Sex and Marriage through the Ages* (New York: Springer Publishing Co., 1974), p. 9.
2. Nena O'Neill and George O'Neill, *Open Marriage* (New York: M. Evans and Co., 1972), p. 38.
3. Nena O'Neill, *The Marriage Premise* (New York: M. Evans and Co., 1977), p. 203.
4. Erica Jong, "Marriage, Rational and Irrational," *Vogue* (June 1975), pp. 94–95.
5. Jong.
6. Cited in Fred McMorrow, *Midolescence* (New York: Times Books, 1974), p. 163.

CHAPTER 5: NOVEMBER-DECEMBER LOVERS

1. Anne Simon, *The New Years* (New York: Alfred A. Knopf, 1968), p. viii.
2. Justin Pikunas, *Human Development* (New York: McGraw-Hill Book Co., 1976), p. 399.
3. Simon, p. 189.
4. Carl Jung, *The Portable Jung,* ed. J. Campbell (New York: Viking Press, 1971), p. 12.
5. Erik Erikson, *Identity: Youth and Crisis* (New York: W. W. Norton & Co., 1968), p. 103.
6. Simon, p. 225.
7. Jolan Chang, *The Tao of Love and Sex: The Ancient Chinese Way of Ecstasy* (New York: E. P. Dutton, 1977), pp. 97–101.

8. Morton Puner, *To the Long Good Life* (New York: Universe Books, 1974), p. 143.
9. Cited in Puner.

CHAPTER 6: THE ODD COUPLES

1. Beth Winship, "Dear Beth," *San Francisco Examiner and Chronicle,* 13 May 1977.

CHAPTER 7: WOMEN ARE LIKE FINE WINE

1. Cited in David Wallechinsky, Irving Wallace, and Amy Wallace, *The People's Almanac* (New York: William Morrow & Co., 1975).
2. Robert Seidenberg, "Older Women and Younger Men," *Sexual Behavior* (April 1972), pp. 9–17.
3. Seidenberg.
4. Cited in Judy Klemesrud, "Women Are Switching Months in May-December Relationships," *The Atlanta Constitution,* 16 April 1979.
5. Judy Klemesrud, "A Look at Romance's 'Last Taboo,'" *San Francisco Chronicle,* 10 April 1979.
6. Francine du Plessix Gray, "The New Older Woman," *The New York Times Book Review,* 15 January 1978.
7. Helen Van Slyke, "Older Women, Younger Men—Why Not?" *Saturday Evening Post* (July 1975), pp. 14–16.
8. Verta Mae Smart-Grosvenor, "Is a Woman over the Hill at 40?" *Ebony* (August 1977), pp. 144–48.
9. Langston Hughes, "Preference," in *Montage of a Dream Deferred* (New York: Henry Holt, 1951).

CHAPTER 8: MY DEAR FRIEND

1. Harvey Cox, "Why Young Americans Are Buying Oriental Religions," *Psychology Today* (July 1977), p. 36.
2. Robert Brain, "Somebody Else Should Be Your Own Best Friend," *Psychology Today* (October 1977), p. 83.
3. Zena Blau, *Old Age in a Changing Society* (New York: Franklin Watts, 1973), p. 68.
4. Beth Hess, *Aging and Society,* vol. 3, ed. M. W. Riley (New York: Russell Sage Foundation, 1972), p. 357.
5. Rudy Haapanen, "Close Friendship: The Individualistic Community," (PhD dissertation, University of California at Davis, 1977).

CHAPTER 10: IS AN AGE-DIFFERENT RELATIONSHIP FOR YOU?

1. George Vaillant, *Adaptation to Life* (New York: Little, Brown & Co., 1977), p. 200.

2. Cited in Judith Thurman, "Jeanne Moreau Talks about Seduction, Aging and Fame," *Ms.* (February 1977), p. 52.
3. Justin Pikunas, *Human Development* (New York: McGraw-Hill Book Co., 1976), p. 396.
4. Adapted from Robert Winch, *Mate Selection* (New York: Harper & Row, Publishers, 1958), p. 91.
5. Don Holloway, "The Development and Testing of a Model for Predicting Physicians' Evaluations of Health Status," (PhD dissertation, University of Wisconsin, 1971).